100 FLOWERS

TO KNIT & CROCHET

100 FLOWERS

TO KNIT & CROCHET

A collection of beautiful blooms for
embellishing garments, accessories, and more

Lesley Stanfield

St. Martin's Griffin
New York

100 FLOWERS TO KNIT & CROCHET.
Copyright © 2009 Quarto, Inc. All rights reserved.
Printed in China. For information, address St. Martin's
Press, 175 Fifth Avenue, New York, N.Y. 10010.

www.stmartins.com

Library of Congress Cataloging-in-Publication Data
Available Upon Request

ISBN-13: 978-0-312-53834-7

First St. Martin's Press Edition: March 2009

10 9 8 7 6 5 4 3 2

Conceived, designed, and produced by
Quarto Publishing plc
The Old Brewery
6 Blundell Street
London N7 9BH

QUAR: FKC

Project Editor: Emma Poulter
Art Editor: Emma Clayton
Designer: Tanya Devonshire-Jones
Copy Editor: Sally MacEachern
Pattern Checker: Susan Horan
Illustrator: Coral Mula
Photographer (directory and technical section): Simon Pask
Photographer (projects): Nicki Dowey
Proofreader: Claire Waite Brown
Indexer: Dorothy Frame
Art Director: Caroline Guest

Creative Director: Moira Clinch
Publisher: Paul Carslake

Color separation by Modern Age Repro House Ltd,
Hong Kong
Printed by SNP Leefung Printers Ltd, China

CONTENTS

FOREWORD

This collection of flowers, fruit, leaves, vegetables, and insects is designed to appeal to anyone who can knit or crochet and everyone who loves flowers. Although the limitations of knitting and crochet have dictated the detail of some of the designs—serious botanists beware—it's a fond, sometimes frivolous, interpretation of the natural world.

The designs are created by simple shapings rather than fancy stitches, so few skills beyond the basic know-how are required, and no wiring is used, so all creations can be handled quite safely by children. Yarn is a lovely medium to work with and the satisfaction of making small objects like these cannot be over-estimated—enjoy!

LESLEY STANFIELD

ABOUT THIS BOOK

This book provides a stunning selection of 100 flowers and natural designs for you to knit and crochet. Each and every one of these gorgeous creations can be used to embellish garments, gifts, accessories, and much more.

SECTION 1: BEFORE YOU BEGIN (PAGES 8–19)
The book begins with some basic knitting and crochet information about yarns, needles and hooks, symbols, abbreviations, and terminology, as well as some notes on how to work the key stitches featured in the book—much of the know-how you need to get started.

SECTION 2: DIRECTORY OF FLOWERS (PAGES 20–45)
The Directory of Flowers is a showcase of the 100 beautiful designs that are featured. Organized into flowers, leaves, and fruit and vegetables, and interspersed with a few insects, the directory contains a mix of crochet and knitted designs. Flick through this colorful visual guide, select your design, and then turn to the relevant page of instructions to create your chosen piece.

Each knitted and crochet flower is labeled with a number that corresponds to the relevant instructions in the Technical Instructions chapter (pages 46–107).

Each design is shown at actual size.

SECTION 3: TECHNICAL INSTRUCTIONS (PAGES 46–107)

Here you'll find instructions on how to create each and every design featured in the Directory of Flowers. Organized into separate knitting and crochet sections, and then subdivided into basic, intermediate, and advanced skill levels, this chapter contains full instructions to aid you in the creation of your chosen design.

All knitted and crochet designs are organized by skill level: basic, intermediate, or advanced.

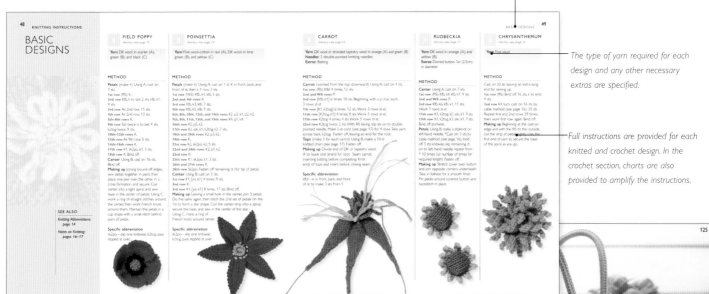

The type of yarn required for each design and any other necessary extras are specified.

Full instructions are provided for each knitted and crochet design. In the crochet section, charts are also provided to amplify the instructions.

SECTION 4: PROJECTS (PAGES 108–125)

The beauty of these designs is that all can be used to embellish a number of items, from garments and accessories, to gift wrap and place settings. This chapter presents a selection of ideas to inspire and encourage you to use the featured designs in a variety of ways—the dilemma is whether to make a flower and then find a use for it, or vice versa!

PROJECT 10: SHOPPING BAG

A vintage plastic shopping bag has been given a new lease of life by tying on a small bunch of colorful vegetables—in this case, knitted carrots and crochet peapods. They could make a flamboyant brooch equally well.

Inspirational ideas on how to apply your knitted or crochet designs are provided.

Each project is illustrated with a photograph of the finished item.

1 BEFORE YOU BEGIN

Before you get started, here is some useful information about yarns, needles, hooks, symbols, and abbreviations, as well as some notes to help you brush up on your knitting or crochet skills.

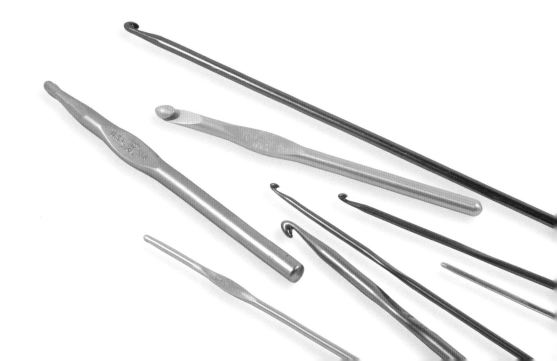

MATERIALS AND EQUIPMENT

Few materials and minimal craft skills are needed for the designs featured in this book. Obviously, changing the type of yarn and color will produce a different result and scale, so it can be very rewarding to experiment.

YARNS

Yarns are available in a range of weights from very fine to very bulky. Because yarns may vary from one manufacturer to another and certainly change from one fiber to another, only generic yarn types are indicated in this book—although smooth yarns are recommended for crochet—and no needle or hook sizes are given. You should be aware of the properties of different yarns, however, from the fullness of cotton to the elasticity of wool, because the construction of a yarn will affect its behavior and characteristics, and so will influence the end result. Experimentation is key. Try using different gauges and, if in doubt, use a smaller needle/hook size than usual.

If you really want to create a florist's shop (or a grocer's counter!) separate your yarns into color groups and keep these in transparent plastic containers so that you have a palette of colors to work with. Don't limit yourself to knitting yarn and look for interesting colors among embroidery threads.

KNITTING NEEDLES

As already mentioned, no needle sizes are specified in this book, but you will want to vary your choice of needle depending on the yarn you are using. Pairs of knitting needles are made in a variety of lengths. Most are aluminum, although larger-size needles are made of plastic to reduce their weight. For most of the designs in this book, a conventional pair of needles is used, but two double-pointed needles are needed to make a cord, and four double-pointed needles where there is knitting in the round. Bamboo needles are available in many sizes.

A variety of different yarn types and weights.

CROCHET HOOKS

Crochet hooks are available in a wide range of sizes and materials. Most hooks are made from aluminum or plastic. Small sizes of steel hooks are made for working with very fine yarns. Hand-made wooden, bamboo, and horn hooks are also available.

Hook sizes are quoted differently in the United States and Europe, and some brands of hook are labeled with more than one type of numbering. Choosing a hook is largely a matter of personal preference. The design of the hook affects the ease of working considerably. Look for a hook which has a comfortable grip.

Pairs of knitting needles, and double-pointed needles, in various materials and sizes.

ADDITIONAL EQUIPMENT

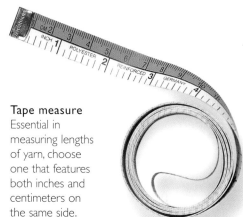

Tape measure
Essential in measuring lengths of yarn, choose one that features both inches and centimeters on the same side.

Markers and row counters
Ready-made markers can be used to indicate a repeat or to help count stitches in a chain (see page 17 for the use of yarn markers). Similarly, a row counter may help you to keep track of the number of rows you have worked, but in knitting this is usually easy if you remember to include the stitches on the needle as a row.

Scissors
Choose a small, sharp-pointed pair to cut yarn and trim yarn ends.

CROCHET SYMBOLS

KEY TO SYMBOLS USED IN CHARTS

BASIC SYMBOLS

◯	Slip ring	◡	Work in the single front strand of the stitch below —this concave curve will appear underneath the stitch symbol.
⬭	Chain		
●	Slip stitch	⌢	Work in the single back strand of the stitch below —this convex curve will appear underneath the stitch symbol.
+	Single crochet		
T	Half double crochet	�	Work around the stem of a stitch—the instructions will indicate whether this is to be done from the back or the front.
⊤	Double crochet		
⊤	Treble crochet	►	An arrowhead indicates the beginning of a row or round where this is not immediately apparent.
⊤	Double treble crochet		

INCREASES

Symbols joined at the base show stitches worked in a single stitch or space to make an increase. They are usually described as "work so many stitches in the next stitch," or at the beginning of a row "work so many stitches in the stitch below."

 2-st sc increase

 2-st dc increase

 3-st dc increase

 2-st tr increase

 3-st tr increase

DECREASES

Symbols joined at the top show stitches gathered into one stitch to form a decrease. Each stitch of the group (dc, tr, etc., according to the symbol) is made without working the last wrap (a wrap is: yarn round hook then pull yarn through loop). This leaves one loop on the hook for each incomplete stitch plus the original loop. The decrease is completed by taking the yarn round the hook and then pulling the yarn through all loops on the hook.

 2-st sc decrease

 2-st dc decrease

 3-st dc decrease

 2-st tr decrease

 3-st tr decrease

 As above, each stitch (one tr around stem of stitch then one dc in next stitch) is worked without making the last wrap, yarn round hook and pull yarn through all 3 loops on hook.

CLUSTERS

A cluster is made exactly like a decrease (see left) except that the stitches are all worked in a single stitch or space before being gathered together at the top.

 2-st dc clusters

 3-st dc cluster

 2-st tr cluster

 3-st tr cluster

 4-st tr cluster

 2-st dtr cluster

ABBREVIATIONS

KNITTING ABBREVIATIONS

k   knit

kfb   knit in front and back of stitch to make two stitches from one

m1   make a stitch by lifting strand in front of next stitch and knit in back of it

p   purl

pfb   purl in front and back of stitch to make two stitches from one

psso   pass slipped stitch(es) over

RS   right side(s)

skpo   slip one stitch knitwise, knit one, pass slipped stitch over

ssk   slip two stitches one at a time knitwise, insert point of left-hand needle into the fronts of these two stitches and knit them together (this is interchangeable with skpo above)

s2kpo   slip two stitches as if to knit two together, knit one, pass the slipped stitches over

sk2po   slip one knitwise, knit two together, pass slipped stitch over

st(s)   stitch(es)

st-st   stockinette stitch

tbl   through the back of the loop(s)

tog   together

wyif   with yarn in front

WS   wrong side(s)

yo   yarn forward and over needle to make a stitch

[ ]   work instructions in square brackets the number of times stated

CROCHET ABBREVIATIONS

ch   chain

ch sp   chain space

dec   decrease

dc   double crochet

dtr   double treble crochet

hdc   half double crochet

inc   increase

sc   single crochet

sp   space

ss   slip stitch

st(s)   stitch(es)

tr   treble crochet

yrh   yarn round hook

( )   round brackets indicate a group of stitches to be worked together

[ ]   square brackets enclose a group of stitches to be worked the number of times stated after the brackets

TERMINOLOGY AND AFTERCARE

AMERICAN/ENGLISH TERMINOLOGY

The patterns in this book use American terminology, which differs somewhat from English terminology. You may find this list of American terms and their English equivalents useful.

AMERICAN

single crochet (**sc**)
half double crochet (**hdc**)
double crochet (**dc**)
treble crochet (**tr**)
double treble crochet (**dtr**)

ENGLISH

double crochet (**dc**)
half treble crochet (**htr**)
treble crochet (**tr**)
double treble crochet (**dtr**)
triple treble crochet (**trtr**)

AFTERCARE

It is a good idea to keep a ball band from each project you complete as a reference for washing instructions, or alternatively make a note of them. Standard laundering symbols are given below, although you may prefer to wash your knitted or crocheted item by hand. This should be gently done in hot water, with a mild, detergent-free cleaning agent. Most purpose-made wool or fabric detergents are ideal, but check the one you choose does not contain optical brighteners which will cause yarn colors to fade. Always rinse the piece thoroughly and allow to dry naturally.

STANDARD LAUNDERING SYMBOLS

Hand Washing

Do not wash by hand or machine

Hand washable in warm water at the stated temperature

Machine Washing

86°F / 30°C
Machine washable in warm water at the stated temperature

86°F / 30°C
Machine washable in warm water at the stated temperature, cool rinse, and short spin

104°F / 40°C
Machine washable in warm water at the stated temperature, short spin

Bleaching

Bleaching not permitted

CL
Bleaching permitted (with chlorine)

Pressing

Do not press

Press with a cool iron

Press with a warm iron

Press with a hot iron

Dry Cleaning

Do not dry clean

A
May be dry cleaned with all solutions

P
May be dry cleaned with perchlorethylene or fluorocarbon or petroleum-based solvents

F
May be dry cleaned with fluorocarbon or petroleum-based solvents only

NOTES ON KNITTING

This section is not a lesson in knitting; it is simply a reminder of a few basics, together with a few suggestions and techniques that might be new to an inexperienced knitter.

SLIPKNOT

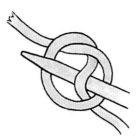

1 Putting a slipknot on the needle makes the first stitch of the cast-on. Loop the yarn around two fingers of the left hand, the ball end on top. Dip the needle into the loop, catch the ball end of the yarn, and pull it through the loop.

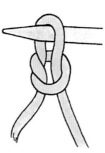

2 Pull the ends of the yarn to tighten the knot. Tighten the ball end to bring the knot up to the needle.

Ends The end of yarn left after making the slipknot should be a reasonable length so that it can be used for sewing up. It can also be very useful for covering up imperfections, such as awkward color changes. The same applies to the end left after binding off. Ends left when a new color is joined in should be darned in along a seam or row end on the wrong side. In these projects, ends left at the tip of petals or leaves will be better darned in before the main making up.

CASTING ON

There are several cast-on methods, each with their own merits.

Long-tail cast-on

This uses a single needle and produces a knitted edge like a row of garter stitch.

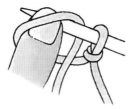

1 Leaving an end about three times the length of the required cast-on, put a slipknot on the needle. Holding the yarn end in the left hand, take the left thumb under the yarn and upward. Insert the needle in the loop made on the thumb.

2 Use the ball end of the yarn to make a knit stitch, slipping the loop off the thumb. Pull the yarn end to close the stitch up to the needle. Continue making stitches in this way.

Cable cast-on

This two-needle method gives a firm result with the appearance of a rope edge.

1 Put a slipknot on one needle. Use the other needle and the ball end of the yarn to knit into the loop on the left-hand needle without slipping it off. Transfer the new stitch to the left-hand needle.

2 Insert the right-hand needle between the new stitch and the next stitch and then make another stitch as before. Continue making stitches in this way.

Knitted cast-on

Make a cable cast-on as above, but instead of knitting between stitches insert the right-hand needle in the front of each stitch in the usual way. This gives a softer edge than the cable method.

DUPLICATE STITCH

Also known as Swiss darning, this is used to make color changes in stockinette stitch after the knitting has been completed. Thread the contrast color on to a wool needle, bring out at the base of one V-shaped stitch, take behind the two threads of the stitch above, bring out in front, and then take down into the base of the stitch. It should cover the stitch exactly. For embroidery and sewing up, use a wool needle. This has a large eye and a rounded point so that it doesn't split the yarn.

CORD

A very useful round cord can be made using two double-pointed needles.

Cast on three (or required number of) stitches and knit one row in the usual way. * Without turning, slide the stitches to the opposite end of the needle. Take the yarn firmly across the wrong side from left to right and knit one row. Repeat from * for the required length.

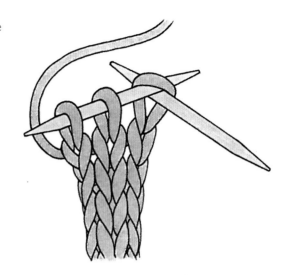

CHAIN

Put a slipknot on the needle. * Knit one stitch. Transfer the stitch just made from the right-hand to the left-hand needle. Repeat from * for the length required. A similar fine chain can be made using a wool needle and starting in the last stitch of a bind-off. Bring the yarn end through the stitch from back to front. Loop the yarn. Insert the needle in the stitch loop from front to back and then in the new loop from back to front. Continue in this way, making loops from left to right and right to left alternately.

MARKERS

If markers are needed to count rows or repeats, use a length of contrast thread. Insert it between stitches from front to back and then from back to front of the work. It can be pulled out when it is no longer needed.

BINDING OFF

Chain bind-off
A simple knit stitch bind-off is used in all these projects, except where a purl stitch bind-off is indicated. Knit two stitches. * With the left-hand needle, lift the first stitch over the second. Knit the next stitch. Repeat from * until one stitch remains. Break the yarn, take the end through this stitch, and tighten.

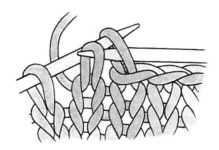

When a row is only partially bound off, the count of stitches to be worked usually includes the stitch already on the needle.

INVISIBLE SEAMING

The neatest way to seam is to use mattress (or ladder) stitch. With right sides facing and starting at the cast-on, take the wool needle under the strand between the first and second stitches of one edge. Repeat at the other edge. Continue working into alternate edges, tightening the stitches as you go, to close up an invisible join.

NOTES ON CROCHET

Understanding how to make simple stitches is the key to constructing interesting shapes in crochet. Here are a few reminders of some basics and some suggestions for building on them.

SLIPKNOT

1 Putting a slipknot on the hook makes the first loop of the chain that will hold the stitches of the first row or round. Loop the yarn around two fingers of the left hand, the ball end to the front. Insert the hook in the loop, catch the ball end of the yarn, and pull it through the loop.

2 Pull the ends of yarn to tighten the knot. Now tighten the ball end to bring the knot up to the hook.

HOOKING ACTION

Hold the slipknot (and later the chain) between the thumb and forefinger of the left hand. Take the yarn over the second finger of the left hand so it is held taut. Take it around the little finger as well if necessary. The right hand is then free to manipulate the hook. With a turn of the wrist, guide the tip of the hook under the yarn. Catch the yarn and pull it through the loop on the hook to make a chain.

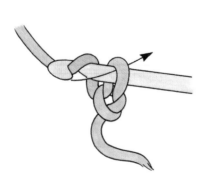

Hooking and catching is referred to as yarn round hook (abbreviation: yrh). It is the action used in making a chain, a slip stitch, and, in various combinations, all other crochet stitches. **Note** Unless the instructions state otherwise, the hook should be inserted under the two strands of yarn which form the front of the chain, or the top of the stitch.

ROUNDS

Rounds are started in a chain ring, or in a slip ring for a tighter center, and are worked in a counterclockwise direction without turning over.

Chain ring Join a number of chain stitches into a ring with a slip stitch in the first chain. Work the first round of stitches around the chain and into the center. If the yarn end is also worked around, the ring is lightly padded and this end can be pulled to tighten it.

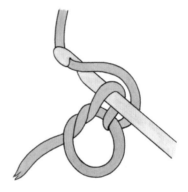

Slip ring

1 To make a slip ring, first coil the yarn around two fingers and then use the hook to pull through a loop of the ball end of the yarn, as if making a slipknot (see step 1, left). However, do not then pull the yarn tight. Holding the ring flat between the thumb and forefinger of the left hand, catch the yarn and pull it through the loop on the hook to anchor it.

2 Working under two strands of yarn each time, make the stitches as directed and then pull the free yarn end to close the ring. Join the ring with a slip stitch in the first stitch.

ROWS

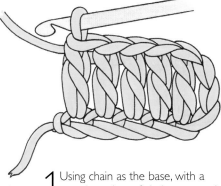

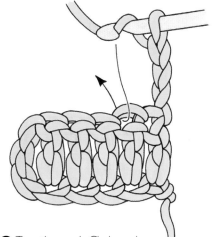

1 Using chain as the base, with a stated number of chain nearest the hook forming the first stitch, work a stitch in each subsequent chain from right to left. The illustration shows a first row of double crochet, with three chain as the first stitch.

2 Turn the work. Chain again forms the first stitch of the next row, but be careful to make the second stitch in the right place. It should go into the next stitch of the previous row and not into the stitch immediately below. Working into the stitch below is the equivalent of making two stitches in the same stitch and results in an increase.

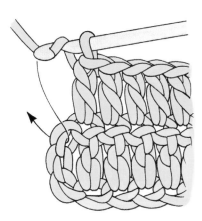

3 The last stitch of a row is made in the top of the chain forming the first stitch of the previous row.

Note Crochet stitches are not symmetrical as the chain that forms the top of the stitch lies to one side of the main part of the stitch (see the illustrations of rows of double above). As a beginner, you may find this disconcerting when first working in rows. Rounds are easier to understand because the stitches all lie in the same direction, usually on the right side of the crochet.

INVISIBLE FASTENING OFF

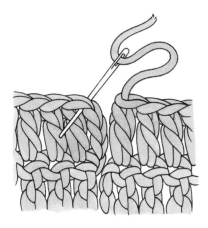

1 For a smooth finish to a final round, simply break the yarn (leaving an end long enough to sew with) and pull it through the loop of the last stitch. Thread it on to a wool needle and take the needle under the two strands of the first stitch.

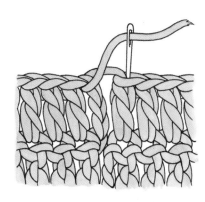

2 Then take it back into the last stitch to form a new stitch, or alternatively pull it tight until it disappears. Fasten off by darning in the yarn end along the chain edge.

2 DIRECTORY OF FLOWERS

Featured here is a collection of stunning knitted and crochet creations. Rifle through the pages of this beautiful directory to find exactly the design you are looking for. Each is labeled with a number that corresponds to the Technical Instructions section (pages 46 to 107). Once you have selected your design, turn directly to the relevant page for full instructions, and begin.

FLOWERS

A vast herbaceous collection of designs, from sprigs through to single blooms. The palette is dictated by the flowers themselves, the names of many—lavender, cornflower, periwinkle, etc.—evoking color. Interpreted in a variety of techniques to look naturalistic or stylized, the flowers are also punctuated with a few insects.

36 TEA ROSE

45 FLARED ROSE

80 FERN LEAF

94 RUFFLED ROSE

68 PELARGONIUM

14 TULIP

62 IRISH ROSE

76 IRISH LEAF

15 CARNATION

16 FLORIBUNDA ROSE

35 PEONY

84 ORANGE-TIP BUTTERFLY

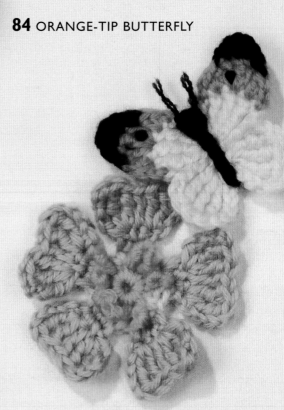

10 SMALL LEAF

64 WILD ROSE

34 ROSE

63 ROLLED ROSE

67 APPLE BLOSSOM

7 LARGE LEAF

63 ROSEBUDS

17 HOLLYHOCK

46 CENTIFOLIA ROSE

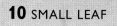
10 SMALL LEAF

31 ANEMONE

65 OLD-FASHIONED PINK

33 ROSEBUD

96 FUCHSIA

95 DIANTHUS

93 ROSETTE

38 COMMON BLUE BUTTERFLY

61 SCOTTISH THISTLE

57 GERANIUM

84 ORANGE-TIP BUTTERFLY

59 AURICULA

10 SMALL LEAF

12 DAHLIA

48 TRADESCANTIA

29 CAMPANULA

60 ASTER

47 MICHAELMAS DAISY

13 CLEMATIS

98 PANSY

56 PERIWINKLE

99 VIOLA

30 PETUNIA

28 LAVENDER

50 MECONOPSIS

27 CORNFLOWER

10 SMALL LEAF

51 BORAGE

69 RED ADMIRAL BUTTERFLY

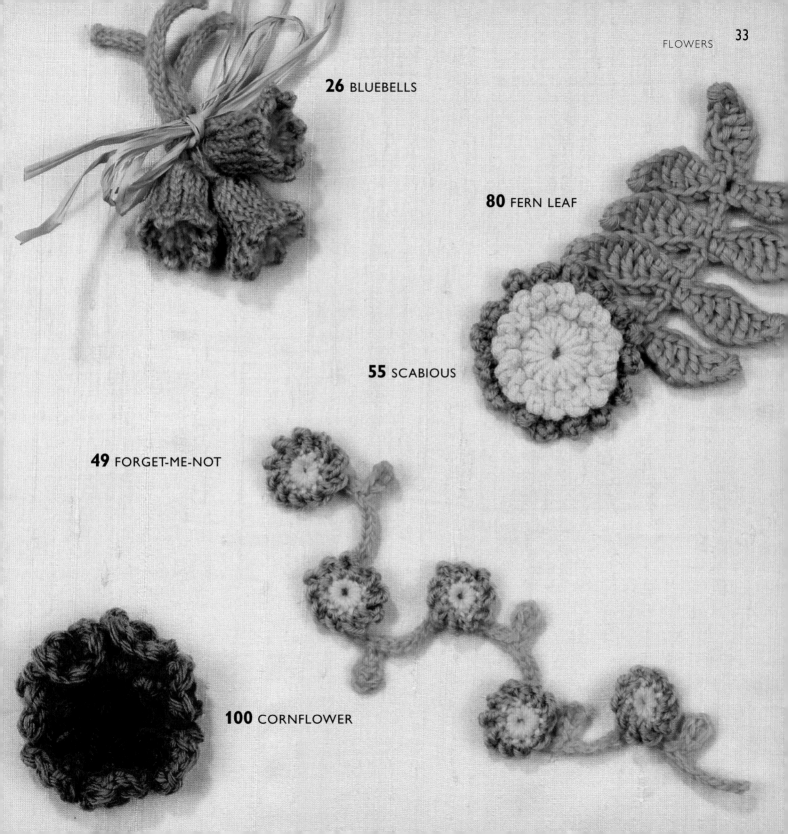

26 BLUEBELLS

80 FERN LEAF

55 SCABIOUS

49 FORGET-ME-NOT

100 CORNFLOWER

2 POINSETTIA

70 BUMBLEBEE

20 CLOVE CARNATION

92 CAMELLIA

91 ORIENTAL POPPY

1 FIELD POPPY

90 HOLLY

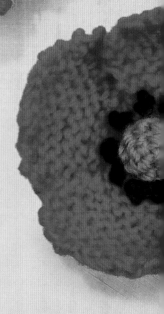

76 IRISH LEAF

5 CHRYSANTHEMUM

82 GERBERA

37 SUNFLOWER

19 LADYBUG

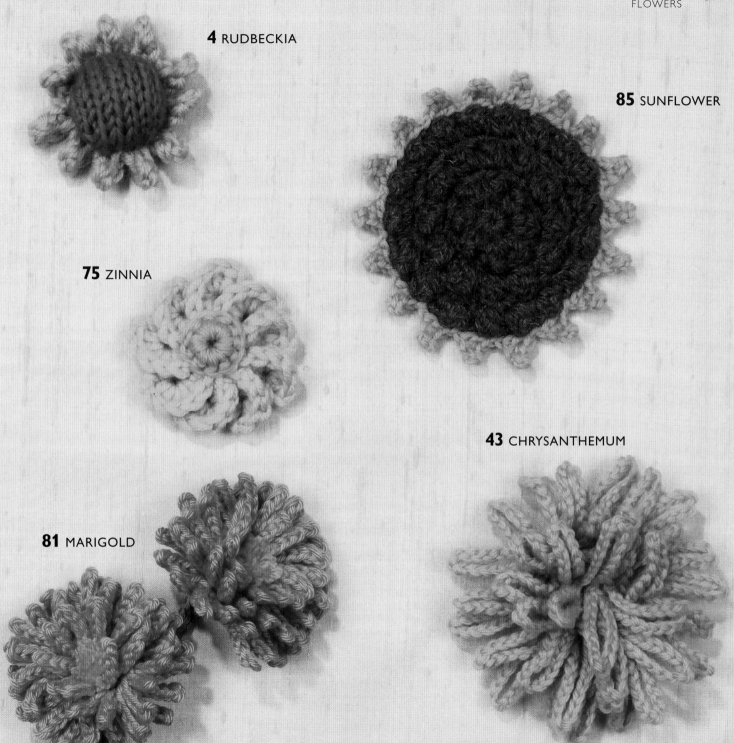

4 RUDBECKIA

85 SUNFLOWER

75 ZINNIA

43 CHRYSANTHEMUM

81 MARIGOLD

83 DAFFODIL

42 BUTTERCUP

83 DAFFODIL

71 NARCISSUS

21 CITRUS LEAF

73 HELENIUM

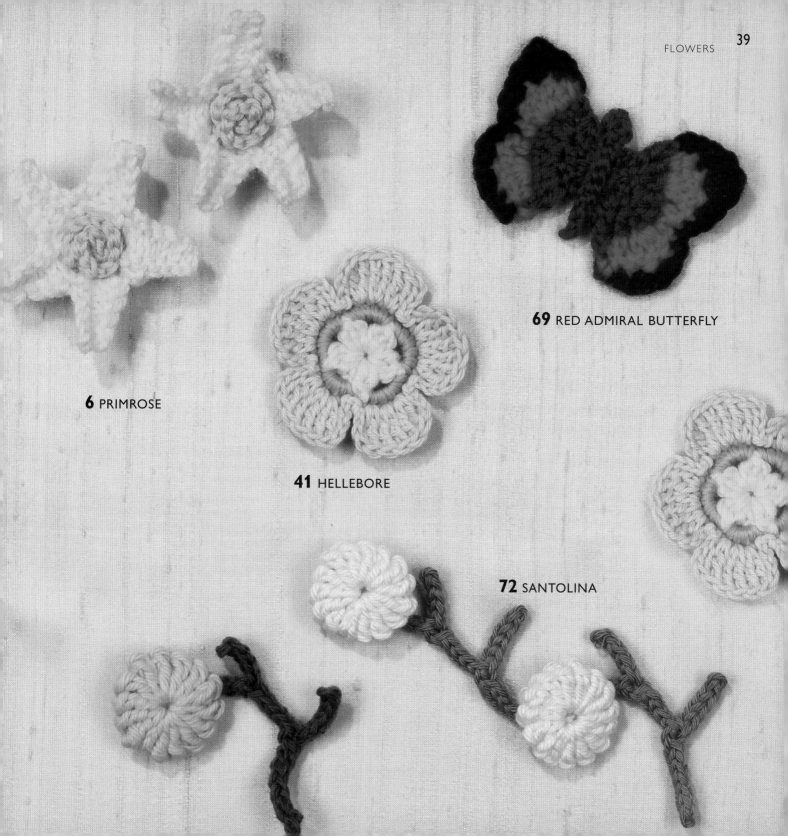

69 RED ADMIRAL BUTTERFLY

6 PRIMROSE

41 HELLEBORE

72 SANTOLINA

54 LILY OF THE VALLEY

25 ARUM LILY

40 MORNING GLORY

74 CAMOMILE

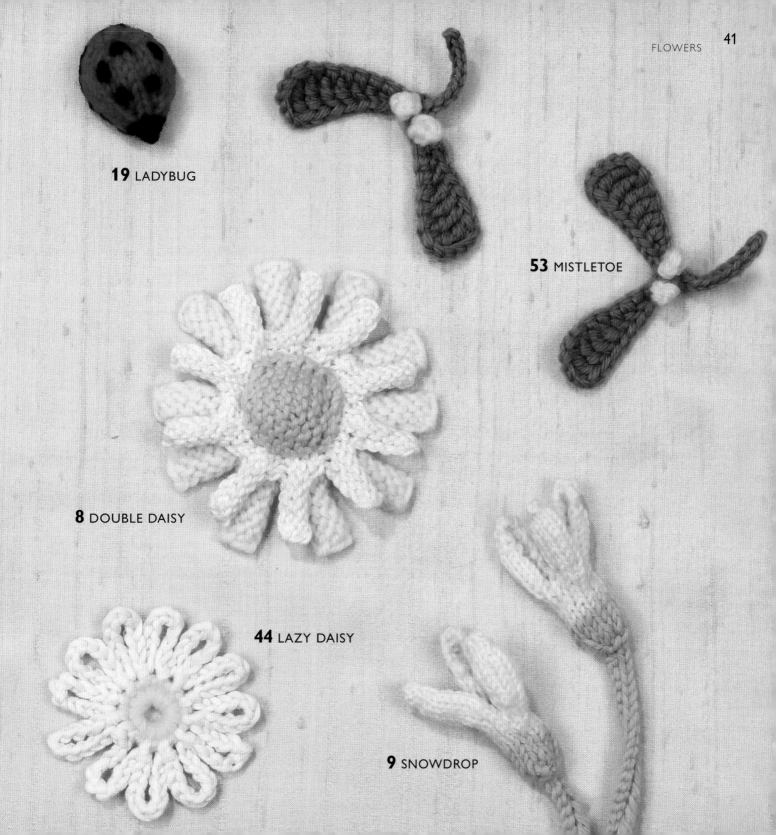

19 LADYBUG

53 MISTLETOE

8 DOUBLE DAISY

44 LAZY DAISY

9 SNOWDROP

LEAVES

From the oak to the citrus, and the ginkgo to the ivy, leaves can be just as interesting as flowers in their shape and design—and they needn't always be bright green. The crochet oak leaf (77) is in two autumnal shades, and the knitted one (22) is in three. With the exception of the holly, most of these leaves could be striped or variegated.

90 HOLLY

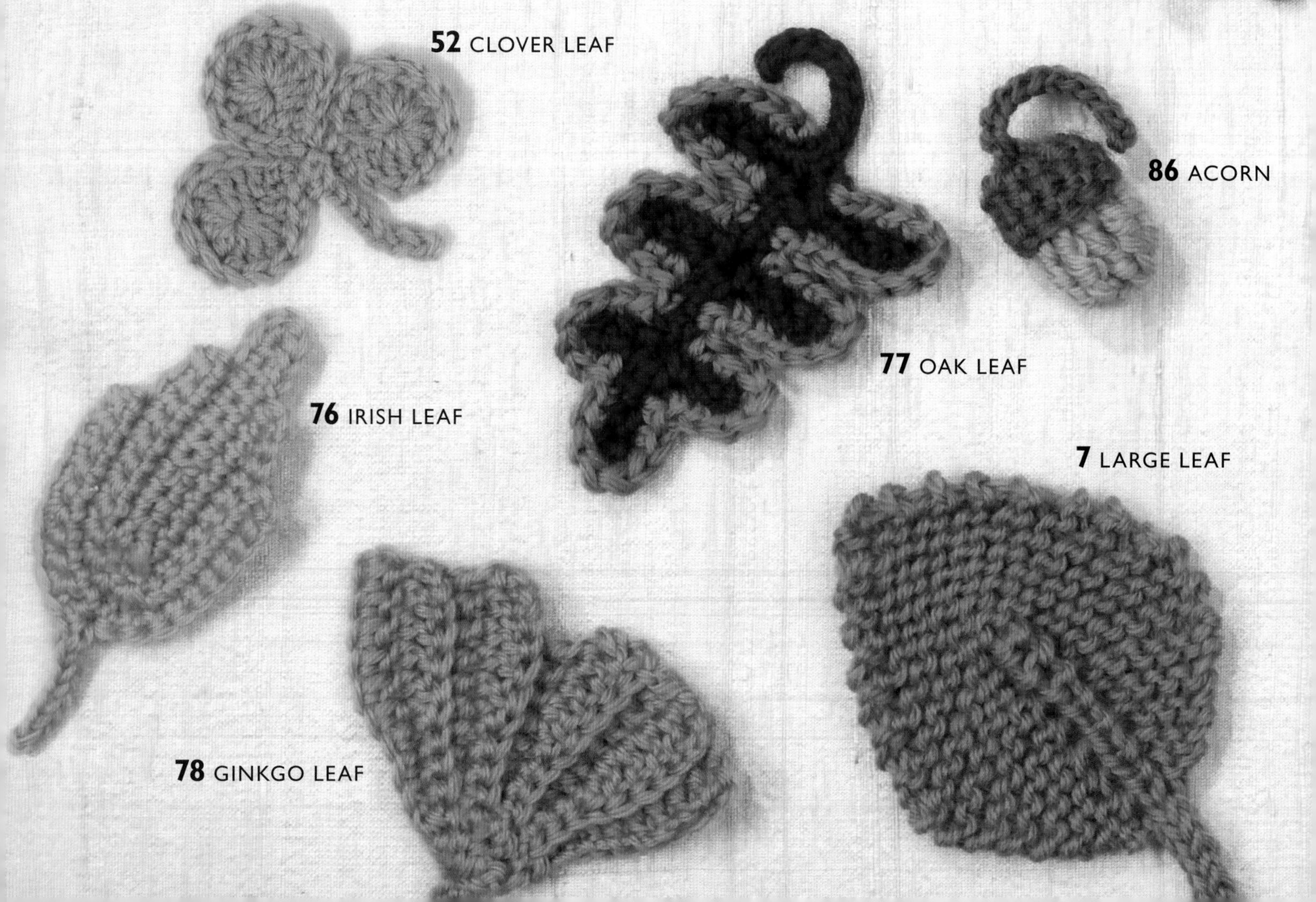

52 CLOVER LEAF

86 ACORN

77 OAK LEAF

76 IRISH LEAF

7 LARGE LEAF

78 GINKGO LEAF

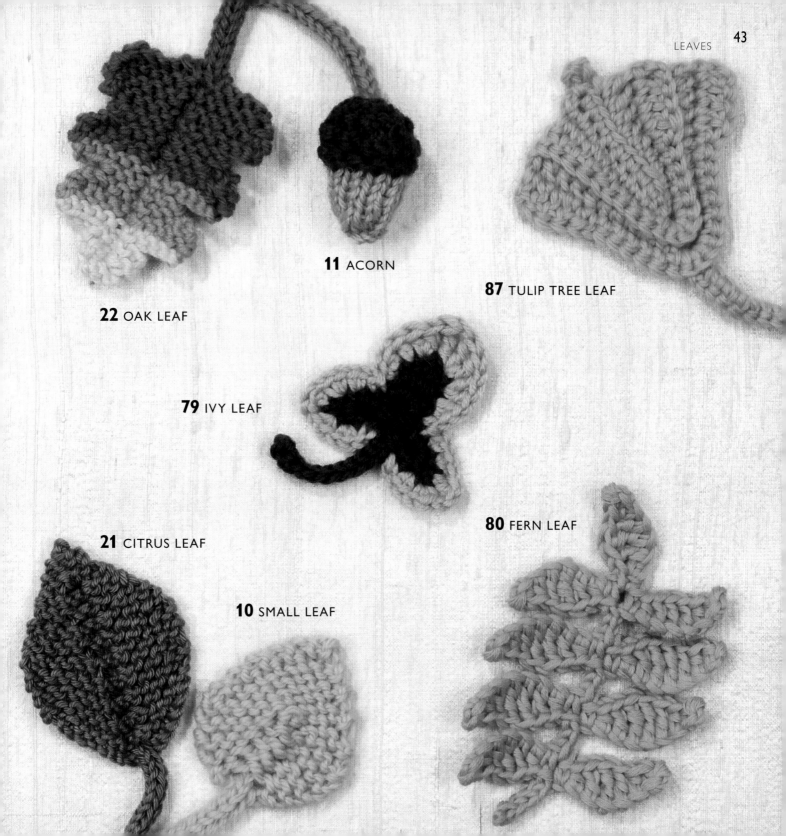

11 ACORN

22 OAK LEAF

87 TULIP TREE LEAF

79 IVY LEAF

80 FERN LEAF

21 CITRUS LEAF

10 SMALL LEAF

FRUIT AND VEGETABLES

The decorative possibilities of fruit and vegetables are many and their colors, some slightly enhanced, can be bright and varied. Perhaps a lemon must always be lemon yellow, but if the radishes were to be made white with mauves they would become turnips. Adapt and enjoy!

32 BLACKBERRY

88 PEAPOD

23 LEMON

21 CITRUS LEAF

24 LEMON BLOSSOM

3 CARROT

89 FIG LEAF

7 LARGE LEAF

18 CHERRIES

97 FIG

58 GRAPES

39 ASPARAGUS

66 RADISHES

3 TECHNICAL INSTRUCTIONS

Organized into knitting and crochet, and ordered by skill within each section, this chapter contains full instructions on how to create all of the designs featured in the Directory of Flowers. For the crochet projects, charts are provided to be used in conjunction with the instructions.

BASIC DESIGNS

SEE ALSO

Knitting Abbreviations:
page 14

Notes on Knitting:
pages 16–17

FIELD POPPY
directory view page 35

Yarn: DK wool in scarlet (A), green (B), and black (C)

METHOD

Petals (make 4) Using A, cast on 7 sts.
1st row (RS) K.
2nd row Kfb, k to last 2 sts, kfb, k1. 9 sts.
3rd row As 2nd row. 11 sts.
4th row As 2nd row. 13 sts.
5th–8th rows K.
9th row Ssk twice, k to last 4 sts, k2tog twice. 9 sts.
10th–12th rows K.
13th row As 9th row. 5 sts.
14th–16th rows K.
17th row K1, sk2po, k1. 3 sts.
18th row K. Bind off.
Center Using B, cast on 16 sts. Bind off.
Making up Joining bound-off edges, sew petals together in pairs, then place one pair over the other in a cross formation and secure. Coil center into a tight spiral and sew base in the center of petals. Using C, work a ring of straight stitches around the center, then work French knots around them. Maintain the petals in a cup shape with a small stitch behind pairs of petals.

Specific abbreviation
sk2po—slip one knitwise, k2tog, pass slipped st over.

POINSETTIA
directory view page 34

Yarn: Fine wool-cotton in red (A), DK wool in lime green (B), and yellow (C)

METHOD

Petals (make 6) Using A, cast on 1 st. K in front, back, and front of st, then k 1 row. 3 sts.
1st row (WS) Kfb, k1, kfb. 5 sts.
2nd and 4th rows K.
3rd row Kfb, k3, kfb. 7 sts.
5th row Kfb, k5, kfb. 9 sts.
6th, 8th, 10th, 12th, and 14th rows K2, p2, k1, p2, k2.
7th, 9th, 11th, 13th, and 15th rows K4, p1, k4.
16th row K2, p5, k2.
17th row K2, ssk, k1, k2tog, k2. 7 sts.
18th and 20th rows K2, p3, k2.
19th row K.
21st row K2, sk2po, k2. 5 sts.
22nd and 24th rows K2, p1, k2.
23rd row K.
25th row K1, sk2po, k1. 3 sts.
26th and 27th rows K.
28th row Sk2po. Fasten off remaining st (for tip of petal).
Center Using B, cast on 5 sts.
1st row K1, [yo, k1] 4 times. 9 sts.
2nd row K.
3rd row K1, [yo, k1] 8 times. 17 sts. Bind off.
Making up Leaving a small hole in the center, join 3 petals. Do the same again, then stitch the 2nd set of petals on the 1st to form a star shape. Coil the center strip into a spiral, secure the base, and sew in the center of the star. Using C, make a ring of French knots around center.

Specific abbreviation
sk2po—slip one knitwise, k2tog, pass slipped st over.

CARROT
directory view page 44

Yarn: DK wool or stranded tapestry wool in orange (A) and green (B)
Needles: 2 double-pointed knitting needles
Extras: Batting

METHOD

Carrot (worked from the top downward) Using A, cast on 4 sts.
1st row (RS) Kfbf 4 times. 12 sts.
2nd and WS rows P.
3rd row [Kfb, k1] 6 times. 18 sts. Beginning with a p row, work 3 rows st-st.
7th row [K1, k2tog] 6 times. 12 sts. Work 3 rows st-st.
11th row [K2tog, k1] 4 times. 8 sts. Work 5 rows st-st.
17th row K2tog 4 times. 4 sts. Work 5 rows st-st.
23rd row K2tog twice. 2 sts. With RS facing, slip sts on to double-pointed needle. Make 2-st cord (see page 17) for 4 rows. Take yarn across back, k2tog. Fasten off, leaving an end for the root.
Tops (make 5 for each carrot) Using B, make a 10-st knitted chain (see page 17). Fasten off.
Making up Divide end of DK or tapestry wool A to leave one strand for root. Seam carrot, inserting batting before completing. Knot ends of tops and insert before closing seam.

Specific abbreviation
kfbf—k in front, back, and front of st to make 3 sts from 1.

RUDBECKIA
directory view page 37

Yarn: DK wool in orange (A) and yellow (B)
Extras: Domed button, 1in (2.5cm) in diameter

METHOD

Center Using A, cast on 7 sts.
1st row (RS) Kfb, k4, kfb, k1. 9 sts.
2nd and WS rows P.
3rd row Kfb, k6, kfb, k1. 11 sts. Work 7 rows st-st.
11th row K1, k2tog, k5, ssk, k1. 9 sts.
13th row K1, k2tog, k3, ssk, k1. 7 sts. Bind off purlwise.
Petals Using B, make a slipknot on left-hand needle. *Cast on 3 sts by cable method (see page 16), bind off 3 sts knitwise, slip remaining st on to left-hand needle; repeat from * 10 times (or number of times for required length). Fasten off.
Making up Stretch cover over button and join opposite corners underneath. Take in fullness for a smooth finish. Pin petals around covered button and backstitch in place.

CHRYSANTHEMUM
directory view page 36

Yarn: Fine wool

METHOD

Cast on 20 sts leaving an extra-long end for sewing up.
1st row (RS) Bind off 16 sts, k to end. 4 sts.
2nd row K4, turn, cast on 16 sts by cable method (see page 16). 20 sts. Repeat first and 2nd rows 29 times, then work first row again. Bind off.
Making up Beginning at the cast-on edge and with the RS to the outside, coil the strip of petals tightly. Use the first end of yarn to secure the base of the spiral as you go.

6 PRIMROSE
directory view page 39

Yarn: DK wool in pale yellow (A) and bright yellow (B)

METHOD

Petals Using A, cast on 8 sts.
1st row (WS) P.
2nd row K.
3rd row Bind off 4 sts knitwise, k to end. 4 sts.
4th row K4, turn, cast on 4 sts. 8 sts.
Repeat 1st–4th rows 4 times, ending with a 3rd row. 4 sts. Bind off, leaving an extra-long yarn end.
Center Using B, cast on 9 sts.
1st row (WS) P.
2nd row K1, [yo, k1] 8 times. 17 sts. Bind off knitwise.
Making up Reverse st-st to the outside, join petals into a ring, and sew bound-off sts to first 4 cast-on sts. St-st to the outside, coil center into a tight ring and secure cast-on base. Insert center in flower and stitch in place.

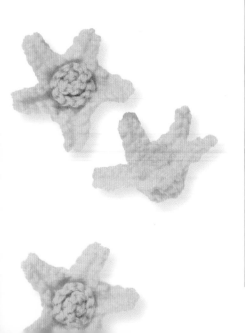

7 LARGE LEAF
directory view page 25, 42, 45

Yarn: DK wool
Needles: 2 double-pointed knitting needles

METHOD

Using 2 double-pointed needles, cast on 3 sts and make a 1¾in (4.5cm) long cord (see page 17). Continue on these sts in rows in the usual way:
1st row (RS) K1, yo, k1, yo, k1. 5 sts.
2nd row K2, p1, k2.
3rd row K2, yo, k1, yo, k2. 7 sts.
4th, 6th, 8th, 10th, 12th, and 14th rows K, working center st p1.
5th row K3, yo, k1, yo, k3. 9 sts.
7th row K4, yo, k1, yo, k4. 11 sts.
9th row K5, yo, k1, yo, k5. 13 sts.
11th row K6, yo, k1, yo, k6. 15 sts.
13th row K7, yo, k1, yo, k7. 17 sts.
15th row K17.
16th and WS rows K.
17th row Ssk, k13, k2tog. 15 sts.
19th row Ssk, k11, k2tog. 13 sts.
21st row Ssk, k9, k2tog. 11 sts.
23rd row Ssk, k7, k2tog. 9 sts.
25th row Ssk, k5, k2tog. 7 sts.
27th row Ssk, k3, k2tog. 5 sts.
29th row Ssk, k1, k2tog. 3 sts.
31st row Sk2po. Fasten off remaining st.

Specific abbreviation
sk2po—slip one knitwise, k2tog, pass slipped st over.

8 DOUBLE DAISY
directory view page 41

Yarn: DK cotton in white (A), fine cotton in white (B), and yellow (C)

METHOD

Lower petals Using A, cast on 9 sts by the cable method (see page 16).
1st row (RS) P.
2nd row K.
3rd row Bind off 5 sts purlwise, p2, turn, with yarn at back slip 1 st purlwise, bring yarn to front, p2. 4 sts.
4th row K.
5th row P.
6th row Kfb, slip these 2 sts on to left-hand needle, cast on 4 sts by cable method, p all 9 sts. Repeat 2nd–6th rows 8 times and then work 2nd and 3rd rows again. 10 petals. Bind off.
Upper petals Using B, work as lower petals.
Center Using C, cast on 5 sts by long-tail cast-on method (see page 16).
1st row (RS) Kfb, k2, kfb, k1. 7 sts.
2nd and WS rows K.
3rd row Kfb, k4, kfb, k1. 9 sts.
4th–10th rows K.
11th row K1, k2tog, k3, k2tog, k1. 7 sts.
12th row [K1, k2tog] twice, k1. 5 sts. Bind off.
Making up Join ends of each strip of petals and lightly gather inner edges of rings, leaving a space in the center. Place upper ring of petals on lower one and stitch together leaving petals free. Padding it slightly with spare yarn, set the center in place and sew on the right side with small running stitches, 1 st in from the edge. Work a few stitches across the space at the back.

9 SNOWDROP

directory view page 41

Yarn: Fine wool in white (A) and pale green (B)

METHOD

Petals Using A, cast on 4 sts.
1st row (RS) Slip 1, k3.
2nd row Slip 1, p3.
3rd row Slip 1, m1, k2, m1, k1. 6 sts.
4th row P.
5th row Slip 1, m1, k4, m1, k1. 8 sts.
Beginning with a p row, work 5 rows st-st.
11th row K2tog 4 times. 4 sts.
12th row P. Break yarn and leave sts on a spare needle. Make 2 more petals.
Base
Next row (RS) Using A, k the 4 sts of each petal. 12 sts. Beginning with a p row, work 3 rows st-st, then change to B and work 4 rows st-st. Bind off, working k2tog along row.
Stem Using B, cast on 18 sts. Bind off.
Making up Do not press. Join side seam of base. Insert stem in opening and secure.

10 SMALL LEAF

directory view page 24, 26, 28, 32, 43

Yarn: DK wool
Needles: 2 double-pointed knitting needles

METHOD

Using 2 double-pointed needles, cast on 3 sts and make a 1¼in (3cm) cord (see page 17). Continue on these sts in rows in the usual way:
1st row (RS) K1, yo, k1, yo, k1. 5 sts.
2nd and WS rows K.
3rd row K2, yo, k1, yo, k2. 7 sts.
5th row K3, yo, k1 yo, k3. 9 sts.
7th row K4, yo, k1, yo, k4. 11 sts.
9th row K5, yo, k1, yo, k5. 13 sts.
11th row Ssk, k9, k2tog. 11 sts.
13th row Ssk, k7, k2tog. 9 sts.
15th row Ssk, k5, k2tog. 7 sts.
17th row Ssk, k3, k2tog. 5 sts.
19th row Ssk, k1, k2tog. 3 sts.
21st row Sk2po. Fasten off remaining st.

Specific abbreviation
sk2po—slip one knitwise, k2tog, pass slipped st over.

11 ACORN

directory view page 43

Yarn: DK wool in brown (A), beige (B), and green (C)
Needles: 2 double-pointed knitting needles
Extras: Batting

METHOD

Acorn Using A, cast on 6 sts.
1st row (RS) Kfb 6 times. 12 sts.
2nd and 4th rows K.
3rd row Kfb 12 times. 24 sts.
5th row K2tog 12 times. 12 sts.
6th row K. Change to B and continue in st-st. Beginning with a k row, work 6 rows st-st.
13th row K2tog 6 times. 6 sts.
14th row P.
15th row K2tog 3 times. 3 sts. Fasten off by taking yarn through all 3 sts.
Stem Using double-pointed needles and C, make a 2in (5cm) long 3-st cord (see page 17).
Making up Taking in 1 st from each edge, seam the acorn from the top, inserting batting and the end of the stem before closing the seam.

12 DAHLIA

directory view page 29

Yarn: DK wool

METHOD

Small petals Cast on 8 sts.
1st row (WS) P.
2nd row K.
3rd row Bind off 4 sts knitwise, k to end. 4 sts.
4th row K4, turn, cast on 4 sts by cable method. 8 sts.
Repeat 1st–4th rows 7 times, ending with a 3rd row. 4 sts.
Do not break yarn.
Medium petals Next row k4, turn, cast on 6 sts. 10 sts.
***1st row** (WS) P.
2nd row K.
3rd row Bind off 6 sts, k to end. 4 sts.
4th row K4, turn, cast on 6 sts. 10 sts. Repeat 1st–4th rows
from * 5 times, ending with a 3rd row. 4 sts. Do not break yarn.
Large petals Next row k4, turn, cast on 8 sts. 12 sts.
**** 1st and 3rd rows** P.
2nd and 4th rows K.
5th row Bind off 8 sts, k to end. 4 sts.
6th row K4, turn, cast on 8 sts. 12 sts. Repeat 1st–6th rows from
** 5 times, ending with a 5th row. Do not break yarn.
Work 10 more medium petals, ending with a 3rd row. 4 sts.
Bind off.
Making up Beginning at the cast-on edge and reverse st-st to
the outside, coil petals, securing them as you go.

13 CLEMATIS

directory view page 30

Yarn: DK wool in purple (A) and yellow (B)

METHOD

Petals (make 6) Using A, cast on 8 sts.
1st row (RS) K2tog, k4, kfb, k1.
2nd row K.
Repeat first and 2nd rows 3 times, then
work first row again. Bind off knitwise.
Center Using B, cast on 12 sts.
1st row (RS) Make a loop on each
st: k1 but do not slip st from needle;
bring yarn over between needles, take
it clockwise around left thumb and
back between needles; k st on left-hand
needle again, slipping it off in the usual
way; on right-hand needle slip 2nd st
over st just made. Bind off, working
k2tog across the row.
Making up Leaving the center open,
join petals to halfway along inner edges.
Pinch a tuck at the inner corner of each
petal and stitch. Join ends of center to
make a ring and stitch it closed. Set
center on petals.

14 TULIP

directory view page 23

Yarn: DK wool in deep pink (A),
pale pink (B), and green (C)
Needles: 2 double-pointed knitting
needles

METHOD

Flower Using A, cast on 43 sts.
1st row (RS) K1, [k2tog, k4, m1, k1, m1,
k4, ssk, k1] 3 times.
2nd and WS rows P.
Repeat first and 2nd rows 5 times.
Using B, repeat first and 2nd rows once
more, then work first row again.
Bind off purlwise.
Stem Using C and double-pointed
needles, make a 4¾in (12cm) long 3-st
cord (see page 17).
Making up Pin out points and press.
Taking in half a st from each edge, join
side seam. On bound-off edge pinch
a fold at point formed by seam. Join
two diagonals of bound-off edge as far
as the increases of last row. Pinch two
remaining points and join the two pairs
of diagonals, leaving a small opening in
center for stem. Insert and attach stem.

CARNATION
directory view page 23

Yarn: DK wool in pink (A) and green (B)
Needles: 2 double-pointed knitting needles

METHOD

Flower Using A, cast on 7 sts.
* 1st row (RS) P.
2nd row Cast on 3 sts by cable method
(see page 16), bind off 3 sts, k to end.
Repeat from * 28 times. Bind off purlwise.
Pin out picot petals and press. With reverse
st-st to the outside, roll remainder tightly and
stitch closed.
Base Using B, cast on 9 sts.
** 1st row (RS) P.
2nd row Cast on 1 st, bind off 1 st, k to end.
Repeat from ** 6 times. Bind off purlwise.
Reverse st-st to the outside, join into a tube
around the base of the petals.
Stem Using B and double-pointed needles,
make a 2¼in (6cm) long 3-st cord (see page
17). Gather the base of the flower around
the top of the stem.

FLORIBUNDA ROSE
directory view page 23

Yarn: DK wool

METHOD

Petals Leaving an extra-long yarn end, cast on 10 sts.
1st row K1, p5, k4.
2nd row K8, kfb, k1. 11 sts.
3rd row K1, p6, k4.
4th and 6th rows K.
5th row K1, p2tog, p4, k4. 10 sts.
7th row Bind off 6 sts knitwise, k to end. 4 sts.
8th row K4, turn, cast on 6 sts by cable method (see
page 16). 10 sts.
Repeat 1st–8th rows 16 times, ending with a 7th row.
4 sts. Bind off.
Center Leaving an extra-long end, cast on 4 sts. Work
38 rows garter stitch (k every row). Bind off, leaving an
extra-long end.
Making up Beginning at the cast-on edge, coil center
into a tight spiral, using the first end to secure it as you
go. Beginning at the cast-on edge and with st-st side to
the outside, coil the petal strip around the center. Use
the first yarn end to secure the petals and stretch the
last few petals so that they are positioned between the
petals of the previous round. End by catching down the
bound-off edge.

HOLLYHOCK
directory view page 25

Yarn: Fine cotton in deep pink (A)
and pale pink (B)
Needles: 4 double-pointed knitting
needles

METHOD

Flower Using A, cast on 6 sts. Slip 2 sts
on to each of 3 double-pointed needles
and continue in rounds:
K 2 rounds.
3rd round Kfb 6 times. 12 sts.
K 2 rounds.
6th round Kfb 12 times. 24 sts.
K 4 rounds.
11th round Kfb 24 times. 48 sts.
K 6 rounds.
18th round Kfb 48 times. 96 sts.
Change to B. K 8 rounds. Bind off.
Making up Press lightly. Fold circle in
half, pinch at center, and roll to form
flower. Catch stitch folds in place.

INTERMEDIATE DESIGNS

18 **CHERRIES**
directory view page 45

Yarn: Fine wool-cotton in red (A) and green (B)
Needles: 2 double-pointed knitting needles, 1 wool needle
Extras: Batting

METHOD

Cherry (make 2) Using A, cast on 12 sts by cable method (see page 16).
1st row (RS) K12.
2nd row P10, wrap 1, turn.
3rd row K8, wrap 1, turn.
4th row P6, wrap 1, turn.
5th row K4, wrap 1, turn.
6th row P to end.
Repeat 1st–6th rows 4 times. Bind off.
Stem Using B and double-pointed needles, and leaving extra-long ends, make two 2in (5cm) long 3-st cords (see page 17).

Making up Seam each cherry and insert batting before closing the seam. Thread a yarn end from one stem on to a wool needle and take it through the center of a cherry, pull it tight enough to shape the cherry, then take it back through to the top and fasten off. Join the 2 stems at the top by knotting the ends and then using them to make a short chain (see page 17).

Specific technique
Wrap 1—to minimize the hole made by turning in mid-row: slip next st purlwise, take yarn to opposite side of work, slip st back on to left-hand needle ready to turn and work next short row.

SEE ALSO

*Knitting Abbreviations:
page 14*

*Notes on Knitting:
page 16–17*

19 LADYBUG

directory view page 36, 41

Yarn: DK wool in red (A) and black (B)
Extras: Batting

METHOD

Upper body Using A, cast on 3 sts.
1st row (RS) Kfb twice, k1. 5 sts.
2nd and WS rows P. **
3rd row Kfb, [k1, m1] twice kfb, k1. 9 sts.
5th row Kfb, k3, m1, k1, m1, k2, kfb, k1. 13 sts.
7th row K.
9th row [K1, ssk] twice, k1, [k2tog, k1] twice.
9 sts.
11th row K1, s2kpo, k1, k2tog, slip st just made
back on to left-hand needle, pass next st over it,
slip st back on to right-hand needle, k1. 5 sts.
Change to B.
12th row P.
13th row K1, s2kpo, k1. 3 sts.
14th row Slip 1, p2tog, psso. Fasten off.
Underside Using B, work as upper body to **
3rd row Kfb, k2, kfb, k1. 7 sts.
5th and 7th rows K.
9th row K1, ssk, k1, k2tog, k1. 5 sts.
11th row K1, s2kpo, k1. 3 sts.
12th row Slip 1, p2tog, psso. Fasten off.
Making up Using B, duplicate stitch 5 spots on
upper body. WS together and cast-on edges
together, use A to join upper body to underside,
inserting batting before closing at head. If any
A stitches show on the underside, cover them
when fastening off B.

Specific abbreviation

s2kpo—slip 2 sts as if to
k2tog, k1, pass slipped
sts over.

20 CLOVE CARNATION

directory view page 34

Yarn: Fine wool in pale pink (A),
mid-pink (B), red (C), and green (D)
Needles: 4 double-pointed knitting needles,
plus crochet hook

METHOD

Flower Using A, cast on 51 sts.
1st row (RS) K1, ssk, * k2, [k1, yo, k1] in next st,
k2, s2kpo; repeat from * 4 times, k2, [k1, yo, k1]
in next st, k2, k2tog, k1. Change to B.
2nd row P.
Continuing with B, work 1st row again.
Change to A, work 2nd and 1st rows.
Change to B, work 2nd and 1st rows.
Change to C, work 2nd and 1st rows.
Using crochet hook, continue with C.
Bind-off row Ss in first st, 3ch, ss in same st,
* ss in next st, 3ch, ss in same st; repeat from
* to end. Fasten off.
Stem Using D and 2 double-pointed needles,
make a 1in (2.5cm) long 4-st cord (see page 17).
Cup Continue with 4 double-pointed needles:
1st round Kfb 4 times. 8 sts. K 5 rounds.
7th round K in front, back, and front of each st.
24 sts. Bind off.
Making up Keeping points of chevron together,
roll lower edge of flower tightly, curving outer
row ends down and stitching in place. Sew on
cup, using yarn ends to fill it out.

Specific abbreviations

ch—chain (crochet);
ss—slip stitch (crochet)
s2kpo—slip 2 sts as
if to k2tog, k1, pass
slipped sts over.

21 CITRUS LEAF

directory view page 38, 43, 44

Yarn: Fine cotton
Needles: 2 double-pointed knitting needles

METHOD

Stem With double-pointed needles, make a 1in
(2.5cm) long 3-st cord (see page 17).
Now work on these 3 sts in rows:
1st row (RS) Cast on 6 sts by cable method
(see page 16), k to last st, p1. 9 sts.
2nd row Cast on 6 sts as before, k to end.
15 sts.
3rd row Kfb, k4, ssk, wyif slip 1 purlwise, k2tog,
k3, kfb, k1.
4th row K. Repeat 3rd and 4th rows 3 times.
11th row K1, ssk, k2, ssk, wyif slip 1, k2tog, k2,
k2tog, k1. 11 sts.
12th and WS rows K.
13th row K5, wyif slip 1, k5.
15th row K1, ssk twice, wyif slip 1, k2tog twice,
k1. 7 sts.
17th row K3, wyif slip 1, k3.
19th row K1, ssk, wyif slip 1, k2tog, k1. 5 sts.
21st row K1, sk2po, k1. 3 sts.
23rd row Sk2po. Bind off remaining st.

Specific abbreviation

sk2po—slip one st
knitwise, k2tog,
pass slipped st over.

22 OAK LEAF
directory view page 43

Yarn: DK wool in olive green (A), ocher (B), and lemon (D)
Needles: 2 double-pointed knitting needles

METHOD

Note A stitch count after a bind-off includes the stitch already on the needle.

Using A and double-pointed needles, make a 1in (2.5cm) long 3-st cord (see page 17). Now work on these 3 sts in rows:
1st row Cast on 5 sts by cable method (see page 16), k7, p1. 8 sts.
2nd row (RS) Cast on 5 sts as before, k6, wyif slip 1 purlwise, k6. 13 sts. On all subsequent RS rows slip the center st in this way.
3rd row K.
4th row K6, slip 1, k6. Repeat 3rd and 4th rows.
7th row Bind off 2 sts, k11. 11 sts.
8th row Bind off 2 sts, k4, slip 1, k4. 9 sts. Work 2 rows straight.
11th row Cast on 2 sts, k11. 11 sts.
12th row Cast on 2 sts, k6, slip 1, k6. 13 sts.
Work 2 rows straight, changing to B on 2nd row.
15th row Bind off 3 sts, k10. 10 sts.
16th row Bind off 3 sts, k3, slip 1, k3. 7 sts. Work 2 rows straight.
19th row Cast on 2 sts, k9. 9 sts.
20th row Cast on 2 sts, k5, slip 1, k5. 11 sts. Work 2 rows straight, changing to C on 2nd row.
23rd row Bind off 3 sts, k8. 8 sts.
24th row Bind off 3 sts, k2, slip 1, k2. 5 sts. Work 2 rows straight.
27th row Ssk, slip 1, k2tog. 3 sts. Bind off.

23 LEMON
directory view page 44

Yarn: Fine cotton
Needles: 4 double-pointed knitting needles
Extras: Batting

METHOD

Cast on 3 sts.
1st row (RS) Kfb twice, k1. 5 sts.
2nd row P.
3rd row K1, [m1, k1] 4 times. 9 sts. Slip 3 sts on to each of 3 double-pointed needles and continue in rounds:
1st round K.
2nd round * K1, [m1, k1] twice; repeat from * twice. 15 sts.
3rd round K.
4th round * K1, [m1, k1] 4 times; repeat from * twice. 27 sts.
K 3 rounds.
8th round * K2, m1, k5, m1, k2; repeat from * twice. 33 sts.
K 3 rounds.
12th round * K3, m1, k5, m1, k3; repeat from * twice. 39 sts.
K 8 rounds.
21st round * K2, k2tog, k5, k2tog, k2; repeat from * twice. 33 sts.
K 3 rounds.
25th round * K2, k2tog, k3, k2tog, k2; repeat from * twice. 27 sts.
K 3 rounds.
29th round * K1, k2tog 4 times; repeat from * twice. 15 sts.
K 1 round.
31st round * K1, k2tog twice; repeat from * twice. 9 sts.
K 1 round. Insert batting.
33rd round * K1, k2tog; repeat from * twice. 6 sts.
34th round K2tog 3 times. Fasten off by taking yarn through 3 remaining sts. Close row ends at the beginning.

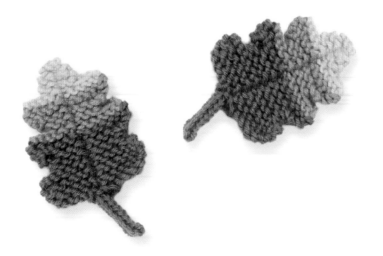

LEMON BLOSSOM

directory view page 44

Yarn: Fine cotton in white (A) and yellow (B)

METHOD

Petals Using A, cast on 4 sts.
1st row K4.
2nd row (K1, p1, k1, p1, k1) in first st, turn, k5, turn, p5, turn, k5, turn, p2tog twice, p1, take yarn to back and on right-hand needle slip 2nd and 3rd sts over first to complete petal, * p2, turn, slip 1, k2.
3rd row P4.
Repeat 1st–3rd rows 3 times, then work 1st and 2nd rows to *. Bind off purlwise.
Making up With st-st to outside, join cast-on and bound-off edges. Slightly gather center. Using B, stitch a ring of small loops around center, anchoring each with a backstitch on WS. Cut loops and trim them.

ARUM LILY

directory view page 40

Yarn: DK wool in pale green (A), white (B), and yellow (C)
Needles: 4 double-pointed knitting needles

METHOD

Stem Using A and 2 double-pointed needles, make a 1in (2.5cm) long 3-st cord (see page 17). Now work one row:
1st row (RS) Kpk in each st. 9 sts. Divide sts, putting 3 sts on each of 3 double-pointed needles and continue in rounds with B:
1st round K.
2nd round [K1, kpk in next st, k1] 3 times. 15 sts. K 4 rounds. Fill this cavity with spare yarn.
7th round [K1, s2kpo, k1] 3 times. 9 sts.
Spathe K 4 rounds, turn. Continue in rows but still using double-pointed needles:
1st and WS rows P.
2nd row K1, [m1, k1] 8 times. 17 sts.
4th row K1, [m1, k1] 16 times. 33 sts.
Beginning with a p row, work 3 rows st-st.
8th row [K2, k2tog] 4 times, k1, [ssk, k2] 4 times. 25 sts.
10th row [K2, k2tog] 3 times, k1, [ssk, k2] 3 times. 19 sts.
12th row [K2, k2tog] twice, k3, [ssk, k2] twice. 15 sts.
14th row K2, k2tog, k2, s2kpo, k2, ssk, k2. 11 sts.
16th row K2, k2tog, s2kpo, ssk, k2. 7 sts.
18th row K2, s2kpo, k2. 5 sts.
20th row K1, s2kpo, k1. 3 sts.
22nd row S2kpo. Fasten off remaining st.
Spike Using C, cast on 10 sts. K 1 row. Slipping first st, bind off.
Making up Insert spike and secure.

Specific abbreviations

kpk—k in front, p in back, k in front of st to make 3 sts from one.
s2kpo—slip 2 sts as if to k2tog, k1, pass slipped sts over.

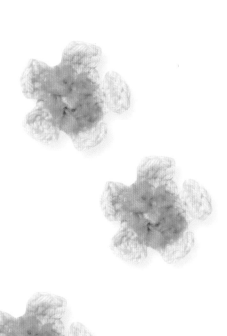

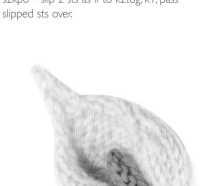

26 BLUEBELLS
directory view page 33

Yarn: Fine wool in blue (A) and green (B)
Needles: 2 double-pointed knitting needles

METHOD

Flower Using A, cast on 15 sts.
1st row (RS) K.
2nd row P.
3rd row [K2tog, yo] 7 times, k1. Beginning with a p row, work 3 rows st-st.
7th row (RS) Join hem: [insert right-hand needle in next st, then in back loop of corresponding st of cast-on row and k2tog] 15 times. Beginning with a p row, work 5 rows st-st.
13th row S2kpo 5 times. 5 sts. P 1 row. Break yarn and run end through sts to gather them.
Stem Using B and double-pointed needles, make a 2¼ in. (6cm) long 3-st cord (see page 17).
Making up Join seam of flower, setting in stem at base. With B, make a small tassel and attach inside flower.

Specific abbreviation

s2kpo—slip 2 sts as if to k2tog, k1, pass slipped sts over.

27 CORNFLOWER
directory view page 32

Yarn: DK wool in deep blue (A), mid-blue (B), and bright blue (C)

METHOD

Center Using A, cast on 4 sts. Do not break yarn.
1st row (RS) Using B, k3, turn, with yarn at back slip 1 purlwise, k2. Do not break yarn.
2nd and 3rd rows Using A, k all 4 sts.
Repeat 1st–3rd rows 9 times, then work 1st and 2nd rows again. Bind off with A.
Petals With RS facing and using C, pick up and k 1 st from each stripe along long edge. 22 sts.
1st row Kfb to end. 44 sts.
Bind-off row * Cast on 3 sts by cable method (see page 16), bind off 5 sts, transfer remaining st to left-hand needle; repeat from *, ending bind-off 4 sts.
Making up Join ends of center into a ring and gather the shorter edge tightly. Pin out petals and press.

28 LAVENDER
directory view page 31

Yarn: Fine wool in mauve (A) and green (B)
Needles: 2 double-pointed knitting needles

METHOD

Flower head (worked from the top downward) Using A, cast on 3 sts.
1st row (RS) Kfb twice, k1. 5 sts.
2nd row P.
3rd row Kfb 4 times, k1. 9 sts.
4th row P.
5th row K1, [cast on 3 sts by knitted cast-on method (see page 16), bind off 3 sts, k1] 4 times. Gently tug each tail to straighten it.
6th row P. Repeat 5th and 6th rows 5 times.
17th row Sk2po 3 times. 3 sts. Change to B. P3. Using 2 double-pointed needles, make a 4in. (10cm) long 3-st cord (see page 17). Bind off.
Making up Working on the RS (see invisible seaming, page 17) and taking in half a st from each side, join the row ends of the flower head.

Specific abbreviation

sk2po—slip one knitwise, k2tog, pass slipped st over.

29 CAMPANULA
directory view page 29

Yarn: Fine wool in blue (A) and green (B), DK wool in yellow (C)
Needles: 4 double-pointed knitting needles

METHOD

Flower Using A, cast on 7 sts.
1st round Slip sts on to 3 double-pointed needles and continue in rounds. K 2 rounds.
3rd round Kfb 6 times, k1. 13 sts. K 4 rounds.
8th round Kfb 12 times, k1. 25 sts. K 6 rounds.
15th round * K2tog, [k1, yo, k1, yo, k1, yo, k1] in next st, skpo; repeat from * 4 times. 45 sts. K 1 round. Bind off.
Stem Using B and 2 double-pointed needles, make a 1in (2.5cm) long 3-st cord (see page 17). Do not break yarn.
Base Using 4 double-pointed needles, work in rounds:
1st round Kfbf 3 times. 9 sts. K 1 round.
3rd round [K2, kfbf] 3 times. 15 sts. K 1 round.
Sepals [K3, turn, p3, turn, s2kpo, fasten off] 5 times.
Making up Sew base to flower and, using ends, catch each sepal to flower. Make 3 double knots on a length of C yarn. Coil and stitch them together, then attach inside bell of flower.

Specific abbreviations
kfbf—k in front, back, and front of st to make 3 sts from one.
s2kpo—slip 2 sts as if to k2tog, k1, pass slipped sts over.

30 PETUNIA
directory view page 31

Yarn: Fine wool in purple (A) and pale mauve (B), DK wool in green (C)
Needles: 2 double-pointed knitting needles

METHOD

Flower Using A, cast on 10 sts.
1st row (RS) Kfb, k6, turn, with yarn at back, slip 1 knitwise, k to end. 11 sts.
2nd row Kfb, k5, turn, slip 1 as before, k to end. 12 sts. Change to B.
3rd and 4th rows K.
5th row Kfb, k4, turn, slip 1, k to end. 13 sts.
6th row Kfb, k3, turn, slip 1, k to end. 14 sts.
7th row K2tog, k4, turn, slip 1, k to end. 13 sts.
8th row K2tog, k5, turn, slip 1, k to end. 12 sts. Change to A.
9th and 10th rows K.
11th row K2tog, k6, turn, slip 1, k to end. 11 sts.
12th row K2tog, k7, turn, slip 1, k to end. 10 sts.
Repeat 1st–12th rows 4 times. Bind off.
Sepals Using C, cast on 6 sts.
* **1st row** (RS) K4, turn, with yarn at back, slip 1 knitwise, k3.
2nd row K5, kfb. 7 sts.
3rd row Bind off 6 sts. Transfer remaining st to left-hand needle, cast on 5 sts by cable method (see page 16), k all 6 sts; repeat from * 3 times, then work 1st and 2nd rows again. Bind off all sts. RS facing, along straight edge pick up and k 3 sts from each sepal. 15 sts. K 1 row.
2nd row Sk2po 5 times. 5 sts. K 3 rows.
6th row K2tog, k1, ssk. 3 sts. Transfer these sts to a double-pointed needle and make a 1¼in (3cm) long cord (see page 17). Bind off.
Making up Pin out petal points and press lightly. Seam to outside, join cast-on and bound-off edges of flower. Darn in ends of A and B along fine stripes on outside. Join base of sepals and attach to base of flower. Using C, make a small knot in center of flower.

Specific abbreviation
sk2po—slip one knitwise, k2tog, pass slipped st over.

31 ANEMONE
directory view page 26

Yarn: DK wool in black (A), white (B), and purple (C)

METHOD

Center Using A, cast on 5 sts.
1st row (RS) [K1, yo, k1] in each st. 15 sts.
2nd row P.
3rd row [Kfb, b1, kfb] 5 times. 25 sts.
4th row P [1A, 3B, 1A] 5 times.
First petal
1st row (RS) K1C, using B kfb twice, k1B, k1C, turn. 7 sts.
2nd row P2C, using B pfb twice, p1B, p2C. 9 sts.
3rd row Using C kfb, k2C, [k1B, k1C] twice, using C kfb, k1C. 11 sts. Continue with C.
4th row Pfb, p8, pfb, p1. 13 sts.
5th row K1, [kfb, k2] 4 times. 17 sts. Beginning p, work 5 rows st-st.
11th row Ssk twice, k9, k2tog twice. 13 sts.
12th and 14th rows P.
13th row K1, ssk, k7, k2tog, k1. 11 sts.
15th row K1, ssk, k1, s2kpo, k1, k2tog, k1. 7 sts.
Working p2tog at each end of row and pulling yarn through last st for a smooth finish, bind off.
2nd, 3rd, 4th, and 5th petals With RS facing, join yarn and work as first petal on each of 5 sts.
Making up Join row ends of center and gather cast-on row. Work a few running sts around each bobble and pull up firmly.

Specific abbreviations
b1—make a bobble: [k1, yo, k1, yo, k1] in next st, turn, p5, turn, k5, slip 2nd, 3rd, 4th, and 5th sts over first st.
s2kpo—slip 2 sts as if to k2tog, k1, pass slipped sts over.

32 BLACKBERRY
directory view page 44

Yarn: Tapestry wool in dark purple (A) and green (B)
Extras: 54 black beads with holes large enough to take yarn; batting

METHOD

Notes Use needles smaller than usual for the yarn weight to make a firm fabric. Thread beads on to yarn before casting on.

Berry (make 1 back and 1 front) Using A, cast on 3 sts.
1st row (WS) Kfb, p1, kfb. 5 sts.
2nd row [K1, b1] twice, k1.
3rd row Kfb, p3, kfb. 7 sts.
4th, 6th, 8th, and 12th rows [K1, b1] to last st, k1.
5th row Kfb, p5, kfb. 9 sts.
7th row Kfb, p7, kfb. 11 sts.
9th, 11th, and 13th rows K1, p9, k1.
10th row K2, [b1, k1] 4 times, k1.
14th row Ssk, [b1, k1] 3 times, b1, k2tog. 9 sts.
15th row K1, p7, k1. Bind off.
Calyx (make 1) Using B, cast on 6 sts.
1st row (RS) Bind off 3 sts, k2. 3 sts.
2nd row K3, turn, cast on 3 sts using the cable method (see page 16). 6 sts.
Repeat first and 2nd rows 3 times, ending with a first row and binding off all the sts on this row.
Making up Sew back and front together, inserting batting before joining bound-off edges at top. With RS to outside, roll calyx and secure cast-on and bound-off edges at straight edge, then sew to top of blackberry.

Specific abbreviation
b1—bring yarn to front, slip next st purlwise, slide bead along yarn so that it sits snugly against work, take yarn to back ready to knit next st.

33 ROSEBUD

directory view page 26

Yarn: DK wool in red (A) and green (B)
Needles: 2 double-pointed knitting needles

METHOD

Petals Using A, cast on 4 sts.
1st and 3rd rows Kfb, k to end.
2nd and 4th rows P to last 2 sts, pfb, p1.
Beginning with a k row, work 4 rows st-st.
9th row K1, k2tog, k to end.
10th row P to last 3 sts, p2tog, p1. 6 sts.
Repeat 1st–10th rows once. 8 sts.
Repeat 1st–10th rows once more. 10 sts. Bind off.
Base Using B, cast on 4 sts.
1st row (RS) P.
2nd row Cast on 3 sts by knitted cast-on method (see page 16), bind off 3 sts, k3. 4 sts.
3rd row P.
4th row K. Repeat 1st–4th rows 4 times. Bind off.
With RS facing, pick up and k 12 sts along straight edge. P 1 row.
Next row K2tog 6 times. 6 sts. P 1 row.
Next row K2tog 3 times. 3 sts. Do not break yarn. Slip sts on to double-pointed needle and make a 1½in. (4cm) long cord (see page 17). Bind off.
Making up Press petals and coil them from the bound-off end, with reverse st-st to the outside. Gather along straight edge and stitch. Join the side seam of base to make a cup and sew bud inside it.

34 ROSE

directory view page 24

Yarn: DK wool

METHOD

Cast on 5 sts.
Small petals
1st row Kfb, k4. 6 sts.
2nd row P4, pfb, p1. 7 sts.
3rd row K7.
4th row P7.
5th row K1, k2tog, k4. 6 sts.
6th row P3, p2tog, p1. 5 sts. Repeat 1st–6th rows 3 times. Do not break yarn.
Medium petals
1st and 3rd rows Kfb, k to end.
2nd and 4th rows P to last 2 sts, pfb, p1.
5th and 7th rows K9.
6th and 8th rows P9.
9th and 11th rows K1, k2tog, k to end.
10th and 12th rows P to last 3 sts, p2tog, p1. 5 sts. Repeat 1st–12th rows twice. Do not break yarn.
Large petals
1st, 3rd, and 5th rows Kfb, k to end.
2nd, 4th, and 6th rows P to last 2 sts, pfb, p1.
7th, 9th, and 11th rows K11.
8th, 10th, and 12th rows P11.
13th, 15th, and 17th rows K1, k2tog, k to end.
14th, 16th, and 18th rows P to last 3 sts, p2tog, p1. 5 sts. Repeat 1st–18th rows twice.
Next row K1, k2tog, k2.
Next row P1, p2tog, p1.
Next row K1, k2tog.
Next row P2tog. Fasten off.
Making up Press. With reverse st-st to outside, roll up loosely from the cast-on end. Lightly stitch the straight edges together to form a flat base, and then push up center. Gather and stitch outside edge at base. Turn back petals and steam if necessary.

ADVANCED DESIGNS

SEE ALSO

Knitting Abbreviations:
page 14

Notes on Knitting:
pages 16–17

35   ## PEONY
directory view page 24

Yarn: DK wool in pink (A) and pale pink (B)

METHOD

Outer petals (make 5) Using A, cast on 6 sts.
1st and 3rd rows (RS) K.
2nd row Kfb 5 times, k1. 11 sts.
4th row [Kfb, k2] 3 times, kfb, k1. 15 sts.
5th–12th rows K.
13th row [K1, k2tog] 5 times. 10 sts.
14th row K.
15th row K2tog 5 times. 5 sts. Leave sts on a spare needle.
To join petals: slip sts back on to working needle, k each set of 5 sts. 25 sts. K 1 row.
Next row K1, [k2tog, k2] 6 times. 19 sts. K 1 row.
Next row K1, k2tog 9 times. 10 sts. Bind off.
Inner petals (make 5) Using A, cast on 4 sts.
1st and 3rd rows K.
2nd row Kfb 3 times, k1. 7 sts.
4th row K1, [kfb, k1] 3 times. 10 sts.
5th–10th rows K.
11th row K1, [k2tog, k1] 3 times. 7 sts.
12th row K.
13th row K2tog 3 times, k1. 4 sts.
Leave sts on a spare needle.
To join petals: slip sts back on to working needle, k each set of 4 sts. 20 sts. K 1 row.
Next row [K1, k2tog, k1] 5 times. 15 sts. K 1 row.
Next row K2tog 7 times, k1. 8 sts. Bind off.
Center Using B, cast on 5 sts.
1st row (RS) K1, * loop 1, k1; repeat from * to end.

2nd row Kfb, k to last 2 sts, kfb, k1. Repeat first and 2nd rows once. 9 sts.
Work 1st row again.
6th row K.
7th row Loop 1, * k1, loop1; repeat from * to end.
8th row K2tog, k to last 2 sts, k2tog.
Repeat 7th and 8th rows once. 5 sts.
Bind off.
Making up Join each set of petals into a ring. Fasten off ends, using those at the base to secure one petal behind the next. Sew the inner petal ring inside the outer one. Gathering it slightly, stitch center in place.

Specific stitch

Loop 1—k1 but do not slip st from needle; bring yarn over between needles, take it clockwise around left thumb and back between needles; k st on left-hand needle again, slipping it off in the usual way; on right-hand needle slip 2nd st over st just made.

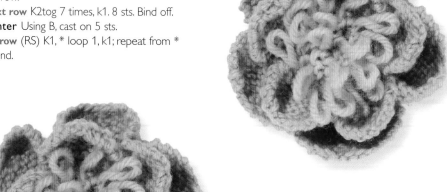

TEA ROSE

directory view page 22

Yarn: DK wool in pink (A) and green (B)
Needles: 4 double-pointed knitting needles

METHOD

First petal (make 2) Using A, cast on 3 sts.
1st row K.
2nd and WS rows P.
3rd row K1, m1R, k1, m1L, k1. 5 sts.
5th row K2, m1R, k1, m1L, k2. 7 sts.
7th row K3, m1R, k1, m1L, k3. 9 sts.
9th row K4, m1R, k1, m1L, k4. 11 sts. **
Beginning with a p row, work 3 rows st-st.
13th row Ssk, k7, k2tog. 9 sts.
15th row Ssk, k5, k2tog. 7 sts.
17th row Ssk, bind off 3 sts, k2tog, slip 2nd
st on right-hand needle over first. Fasten off.
3rd and 4th petals Work as first petal to
**. Work 5 rows st-st, then complete as
first petal.
5th and 6th petals Work as first petal
to **. Work 7 rows st-st, then complete
as first petal.
Stem Using B and 2 double-pointed
needles, make a 1¼in (3cm) long 3-st cord
(see page 17).
Cup With 4 double-pointed needles:
1st round Kpk 3 times. 9 sts. K 4 rounds.
6th round Sk2po 3 times. 3 sts.
7th round [K1, yo, k1, yo, k1] in each of 3 sts.
15 sts.

First sepal
1st row (RS) K5, turn.
2nd and 4th rows P.
3rd row Ssk, k1, k2tog. 3 sts.
5th row Sk2po. Fasten off.
2nd and 3rd sepals With RS facing,
join yarn and work as first sepal on each
of 5 sts.
Making up Roll first petal tightly and secure.
Arrange other petals in a spiral around this,
stitching each in turn. Extend point of each
sepal by unfastening last st and working a few
chain sts. Stitch cup in place.

Specific abbreviations

kpk—k in front, p in back, k in front of st to
make 3 sts from one.
m1L—with tip of left-hand needle, lift strand
between sts so that it lies the same way as
other sts, and k in back of it.
m1R—with tip of left-hand needle, lift strand
between sts so that it lies the opposite way
to other sts, and k in front of it.
sk2po—slip one st knitwise, k2tog, pass
slipped stitch over.

SUNFLOWER

directory view page 37

Yarn: DK wool in khaki (A) and yellow (B)

METHOD

Center Using A, cast on 5 sts.
1st row (RS) Kpk, p1, k1, pkp, k1. 9 sts.
2nd, 3rd, and 4th rows K1, * p1, k1; repeat from *
to end.
5th row Kpk, [p1, k1] 3 times, pkp, k1. 13 sts.
6th–14th rows As 2nd row.
15th row K1, p3tog, [k1, p1] twice, k1, p3tog, k1. 9 sts.
16th, 17th, and 18th rows As 2nd row.
Bind off, working k1, p3tog, k1, p3tog, k1 across row.
Petals With RS facing and using B, pick up and k 1 st
from edge, transfer this st to left-hand needle, cast on
3 sts by knitted cast-on method (see page 16), bind
off 3 sts, * pick up and k 1 st from edge, slip st already
on right-hand needle over it then transfer new st to
left-hand needle, cast on 3 sts as before, bind off 3 sts;
repeat from * around edge. Fasten off.

Specific abbreviations

kpk—(k in front, p in front, k in back) of st to make 3
sts from one.
pkp—(p in front, k in back, p in front) of st to make 3
sts from one.

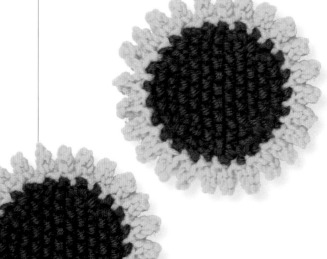

38 COMMON BLUE BUTTERFLY
directory view page 27

Yarn: DK wool in pale blue (A) and deep blue (B)
Needles: 2 double-pointed knitting needles

METHOD

Right upper wing Using A, cast on 4 sts.
1st row (RS) Kfb 3 times, k1. 7 sts.
2nd row P1tbl, [k1, p1tbl] 3 times.
3rd row K1tbl, [p1, k1tbl] 3 times. Repeat 2nd and 3rd rows (rib) 3 times. *
10th row (WS) Rib 5, turn, slip 1 purlwise, rib to end.
11th row Rib 3, turn, slip 1 purlwise, rib to end. ** Break yarn. Slip sts on to other needle. With RS facing and using B, working in back strand only of sts at row ends, pick up and k one st from shorter side edge, k 7 from needle, pick up and k 3 sts from longer side edge. (If necessary, pick up side edge sts on separate needle, then slip them on to working needle.) 11 sts.
Slipping first st, bind off loosely knitwise.
Right lower wing RS facing and using A, working in back strand only and starting at first row, pick up and k 5 sts along first half of shorter edge of upper wing.
1st row Pfkb in first st, p1tbl, k1, pfkb in next st, p1tbl. 7 sts.
2nd row K1tbl, [p1, k1tbl] 3 times.
3rd row P1tbl, [k1, p1tbl] 3 times. Repeat 2nd and 3rd rows once.
6th row (RS) Rib 5, turn, slip 1 purlwise, rib 2, turn, slip 1 purlwise, rib to end. Break yarn. Slip sts on to other needle. With RS facing and using B, working in back strand at row ends, pick up and k 2 sts from side edge, k7 from needle, pick up and k 2 sts from 2nd side edge. 11 sts. Bind off as before.
Left upper wing Work as right upper wing to *, then work 2nd row again.
11th row (RS) Rib 5, turn, slip 1 purlwise, rib to end.
12th row Rib 3, turn, slip 1 purlwise, rib to end. Continue as right upper wing from **, picking up 3 sts from longer side edge and one st from shorter edge.
Left lower wing Work to match right lower wing, picking up sts along second half of shorter edge of upper wing.
Body Using B and double-pointed needles, cast on 2 sts. Kfb twice, turn, p2tog twice, turn. Now make a 1¼in. (3cm) long 2-st cord (see page 17). Skpo. Fasten off.
Making up Press to shape. Join pairs of wings in center and attach body. Use single strands of B for antennae.

Specific abbreviation
pfkb—purl in front then k in back of st to make 2 sts from one.

39 ASPARAGUS
directory view page 45

Yarn: DK wool in white (A), pale green (B), and mauve (C)
Needles: 4 double-pointed knitting needles
Extras: Batting

METHOD

Stalk Using A, cast on 9 sts. Slip 3 sts on to each of 3 double-pointed needles and continue in rounds of k. Work 1in (2.5cm) ending between needles. Do not break yarn. Change to B.
First bract K 3 sts on next needle, turn, p3, turn, s2kpo. Fasten off. Resume A and, working into A sts behind and beneath first row of B sts, pick up and k 3 sts. Continue on all 9 sts, working bracts on each needle in turn and at approximately 1in (2.5cm) intervals until work measures 5in (13cm). Break off A and continue with B.
Tip of asparagus * (K1, m1, k1, m1, k1) in next 3 sts, turn. Continue on these 5 sts: p5, k5, p5, turn.
Next row (RS) K2tog, k1, ssk. P3.
Next row S2kpo. Fasten off remaining st. Repeat from * twice. Using B, pick up and k 3 sts from behind each bract as before. Continue in rounds on these 9 sts. K 2 rounds.
3rd round [K1, m1, k1, m1, k1 in next 3 sts] 3 times. 15 sts.
K 3 rounds. Change to C.
7th round [K2tog, k1, ssk] 3 times. 9 sts. K 1 round.
Fill tip with batting and yarn ends.
9th round S2kpo 3 times. Fasten off by threading end through remaining 3 sts.
Making up Catch down tips of bracts using ends. Use a pencil to push batting into stalk. Close base of stalk by weaving end across opening.

Specific abbreviation
s2kpo—slip 2 sts as if to k2tog, k1, pass slipped sts over.

MORNING GLORY

directory view page 40

Yarn: Fine wool in white (A) and green (B)
Needles: 4 double-pointed knitting needles

METHOD

Flower Using A, cast on 5 sts. Slip sts on to 3 double-pointed needles and continue in rounds: K 1 round.
2nd round Kfb 5 times. 10 sts. K 4 rounds.
7th round Kfb 10 times. 20 sts. K 8 rounds.
16th round [K1, kfb] 10 times. 30 sts. K 4 rounds.
21st round [K2, kfb] 10 times. 40 sts. K 2 rounds.
24th round [K3, kfb] 10 times. 50 sts. K 2 rounds.
27th round [K4, kfb] 10 times. 60 sts. K 3 rounds.
Bind-off round Bind off 5 sts, * return st on right-hand needle to left-hand needle and cast on 2 sts **, bind off 8 sts ***, repeat from * to *** 8 times, repeat from * to **, bind off 2 sts. Fasten off.
Center Using B, cast on 1 st.
1st row [K1, yo, k1, yo, k1] in 1 st. 5 sts. Beginning with a p row, work 2 rows st-st.
4th row P5tog. Fasten off.
Stem Using B and 2 double-pointed needles, make a 1¾in (4.5cm) long 4-st cord (see page 17). Do not break yarn.
Sepals [K1, yo, k1, yo, k1, yo, k1] in each st, turn. 28 sts. Bind off.
Making up Sew center inside flower and join sepals to flower.

Leaf Using B and pair of knitting needles, cast on 3 sts.
1st row K.
2nd and WS rows P.
3rd row Kfb twice, k1. 5 sts.
5th row K1, kfb twice, k2. 7 sts.
7th row K2, kfb twice, k3. 9 sts.
9th row K3, kfb twice, k4. 11 sts.
11th row K4, kfb twice, k5. 13 sts.
13th row K5, kfb twice, k6. 15 sts.
15th row K6, kfb twice, k7. 17 sts.
17th row K7, kfb twice, k8. 19 sts.
19th row K8, kfb twice, k9. 21 sts.
21st row K3, slip 1 knitwise twice, * lift 2nd st on left-hand needle over first st and slip this st purlwise, lift 2nd slip st on right-hand needle over purlwise slip st and return st to left-hand needle **; repeat from * once **, k2, kfb twice, k3; slip 1 knitwise twice, repeat from * to ** twice, k3. 15 sts.
First side
Next row (WS) P7, turn.
Next row K1, slip 1 knitwise twice, repeat from * to ** of 21st row twice, k2. 3 sts. Bind off. With WS facing, slip center st and work 2nd side as first side on remaining 7 sts.
Stem Join B to center st and make 6 chain sts (see page 17). Fasten off.
Making up Join leaf stem to flower stem, darning end in chain to strengthen leaf stem.

BASIC DESIGNS

Yarn: Fine cotton in yellow (A), ocher (B), and pale green (C)

METHOD

Center Using A, make 5ch, join with ss into a ring.

1st round (RS) 3ch, 2-st dc cluster, 2ch, [3-st dc cluster, 2ch] 4 times, with B ss to top ch of 3ch. 5 clusters and 5 ch sp. Continue with B.

2nd round [5sc in ch sp] 5 times, with C ss to first sc. 25 sts. Continue with C.

3rd round [Ss in next sc, 3ch, 2tr in each of next 3sc, 3ch, ss in next sc] 5 times, ss to first ss. Fasten off invisibly (see page 19).

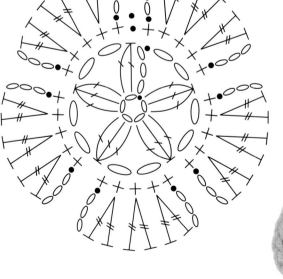

STITCH KEY	SEE ALSO

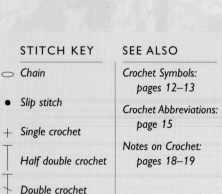

STITCH KEY

⊖ *Chain*

● *Slip stitch*

+ *Single crochet*

T *Half double crochet*

╤ *Double crochet*

╪ *Treble crochet*

╪╪ *Double treble crochet*

SEE ALSO

Crochet Symbols:
   pages 12–13

Crochet Abbreviations:
   page 15

Notes on Crochet:
   pages 18–19

42 BUTTERCUP
directory view page 38

Yarn: Fine cotton in green (A), lime (B), and yellow (C)

METHOD

Using A, make 4ch, join with ss into a ring.
1st round (RS) 1ch, 4sc in ring, with B ss in 1ch. 5 sts. Continue with B.
2nd round 1ch, 2sc in ch below, 3sc in each of next 4sc, with C ss in 1ch. 15 sts. Continue with C.
3rd round [2ch, 2-dc dec in next 2sc, 2ch, ss in next sc] 5 times, ending ss in ss of previous round. Fasten off invisibly (see page 19).

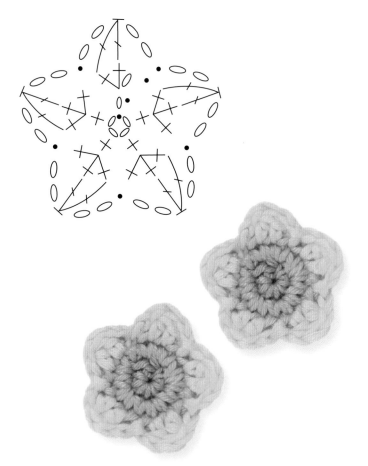

43 CHRYSANTHEMUM
directory view page 37

Yarn: DK wool

METHOD

Make 4ch.
1st double row Skip 2ch, 1sc in each of next 2ch, 17ch, turn, 1sc in each of 2sc, 1sc in top ch of 2ch.
2nd double row 1ch, 1sc in each of next 2ch, 17ch, turn, 1sc in each of 2sc, 1sc in 1ch. Repeat 2nd double row 34 times. Fasten off.
Making up Pin out loops and press. Coil the straight edge, stitching as you go.

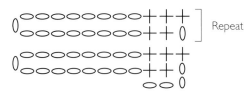

Repeat

44

LAZY DAISY
directory view page 41

Yarn: DK cotton in yellow (A) and white (B)

METHOD

Center Using A, make 6ch, join with ss into a ring.
1st round (RS) 1ch, 11sc in ring, using B ss in 1ch. 12 sts.
Petals Continue with B.
2nd round [11ch, ss in next sc] 12 times, ending ss in ss of first round.
Fasten off invisibly (see page 19).

45

FLARED ROSE
directory view page 22

Yarn: DK wool

METHOD

Leaving a long end of yarn, make 48ch.
1st row (RS) Skip 4ch, 1tr in each of next 43ch, 1dc in last ch. 45 sts.
2nd row 3ch, 3tr in each of next 43tr, 1dc in top ch of 4ch. Fasten off, leaving a long end.
Making up Extend increase edge (2nd row) and press. Coil chain edge counterclockwise, starting with the beginning of the first row and using the long end to stitch as you go. When the coil is completed, catch the yarn end of the 2nd row and take it down through the center of the rose.

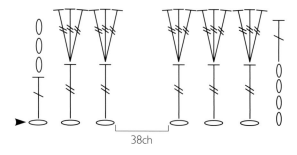

38ch

46 CENTIFOLIA ROSE

directory view page 25

Yarn: DK wool in deep pink (A) and pale pink (B)

METHOD

Using A, make 99ch.

Petals 1–4 Skip 3ch, 1dc in each of next 2ch, 2ch, ss in next ch, [3ch, 1dc in each of next 2ch, 2ch, ss in next ch] 3 times. Continue with B.

Petals 5–8 [4ch, 1tr in each of next 4ch, 3ch, ss in next ch] 4 times.

Petals 9–12 [4ch, 1tr in each of next 6ch, 3ch, ss in next ch] 4 times.

Petals 13–16 [5ch, 1dtr in each of next 8ch, 4ch, ss in next ch] 4 times. Fasten off.

Making up Press petals to shape. Starting with the smaller petals and stitching as you go, coil the row of petals to give a flat base along the chain edge.

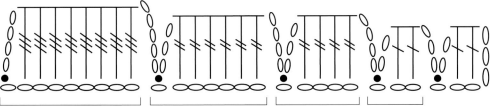

Repeat   Repeat   Repeat   Repeat

Small rose

Using B, make 48ch.

Petals 1–3 as petals 1–4 above, but work instructions in square brackets twice.

Petals 4–6 as petals 5–8, but work instructions in square brackets 3 times.

Petals 7–9 as petals 9–12, but work instructions in square brackets 3 times.

Making up As above.

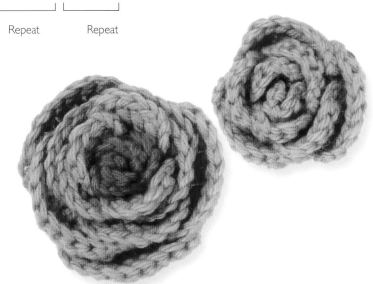

47 MICHAELMAS DAISY
directory view page 30

Yarn: Fine wool in mauve (A) and green (B)

METHOD

Petals Using A, [make 9ch, skip 1ch, ss in each of next 8ch] 37 times. Fasten off. Pin out row of petals and press.

Center With same side facing and using B, join yarn in the space between first and 2nd petals, 3ch, 3-st dc dec in next 3 spaces, * 4-st dc dec in next 4 spaces; repeat from * to end. Fasten off, leaving a long end.

Making up Coil the center so that there are 3 layers of petals. Gathering center slightly, stitch in place. Take yarn end from center and make stem: 15ch, skip 1ch, ss in each of next 14ch. Fasten off.

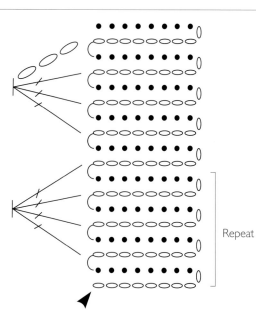

Repeat

48 TRADESCANTIA
directory view page 29

Yarn: DK wool in yellow (A) and purple (B)

METHOD

Using A, make 4ch, join with ss into a ring.
1st round (RS) 3ch, [1sc, 2ch] twice in ring, with B ss to first of 3ch.
3 sts and 3ch sp. Continue with B.
2nd round [4ch, 3-st tr cluster in ch sp, 4ch, 1sc in top of cluster; 4ch, ss in next sc of first round] 3 times, ending ss in ss of first round. Fasten off.

49 FORGET-ME-NOT
directory view page 33

Yarn: Fine wool in yellow (A), blue (B), and green (C)

METHOD

Flower Using A, make 4ch, join with ss into a ring.
1st round (RS) 2ch, 9sc in ring, with B ss to top ch of 2ch. 10 sts.
Continue with B.
2nd round 5ch, 1dtr in each of next 9sc, ss to top ch of 5ch.
Fasten off.
Stem Using C, make 12ch, skip 1ch, ss in each of next 7ch, **leaf:** 5ch, skip 2ch, 1dc in next ch, 1sc in next ch, ss in next ch; ss in each of remaining 4ch. Fasten off.
Making up Press stem and leaf only then attach to back of flower.

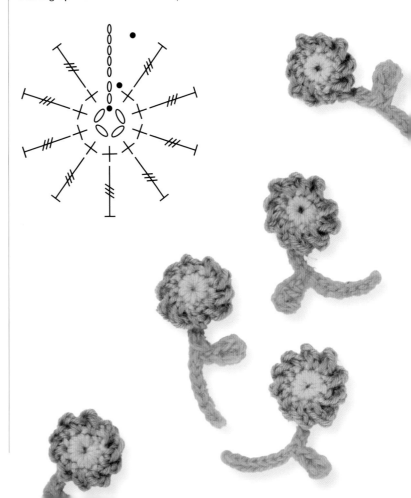

50 MECONOPSIS
directory view page 32

Yarn: DK wool in yellow (A) and blue (B)

METHOD

Using A, make 6ch, join with ss into a ring.
1st round (RS) 1ch, 9sc in ring, with B ss to 1ch. 10 sts. Continue with B.
2nd round [4ch, 2-st tr cluster in next sc, 4ch, 1sc in next sc] 5 times, ending ss in 1ch of first round. Fasten off invisibly (see page 19).

51 BORAGE
directory view page 32

Yarn: DK wool in shades of blue (A) and pale green (B)

METHOD

Flower (make 7) Using A, make 6ch, join with ss into a ring,
1st round (RS) [2ch, 2dc, 2ch, ss in ring] 4 times. 4 petals. Fasten off.
2nd round Using B, join yarn between petals, [1sc between petals and into ring, 1ch behind petal] 4 times, ss in back of first sc, make 10ch for stem. Fasten off invisibly (see page 19).

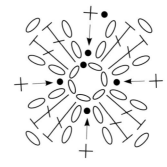

+ **Specific symbol**
↓ 1sc worked over sc and
↓ ring, into center space.

CLOVER LEAF
directory view page 42

Yarn: Fine wool

METHOD

First lobe Make 5ch. RS facing, skip 2ch, 1sc in next ch, 1dc in next ch, 10tr in last ch; working in remaining strand of each ch: 1dc in next ch, 1sc in next ch, ss in next ch. Fasten off.

Make two more the same but without fastening off the last one.

Stem Using attached yarn and with RS facing, make 9ch, skip 1ch, ss in each of next 8ch, ss in first st of attached lobe, ss in first st of 2nd lobe, ss in first st of first lobe, ss in 8th ss of stem. Fasten off invisibly (see page 19).

MISTLETOE
directory view page 41

Yarn: DK wool in green (A) and white (B)

METHOD

Leaves (RS) Using A, * make 14ch, skip 5ch, 1dtr in each of next 2ch, 1tr in each of next 2ch, 1dc in each of next 2ch, 1hdc in next ch, 1sc in each of next 2ch; repeat from * once, ss in remaining strand of first ch. Do not fasten off.

Stem Make 9ch, skip 1ch, ss in each of next 8ch. Fasten off invisibly (see page 19).

Berry (make 2) Using B, make 2ch, skip 1ch, (1dc, 1sc) in next ch. Fasten off invisibly.

Making up Press leaves. Tie both yarn ends of each berry, then sew on to leaves.

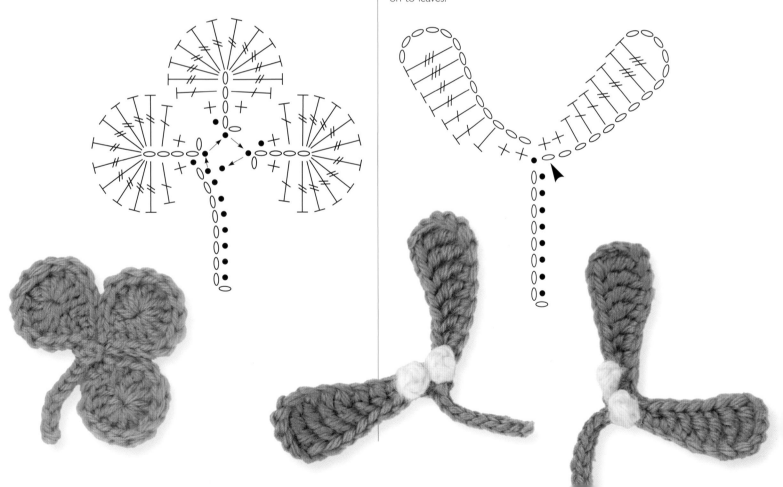

INTERMEDIATE DESIGNS

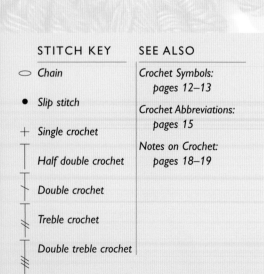

 54

LILY OF THE VALLEY

directory view page 40

Yarn: Fine cotton in white (A) and green (B)

METHOD

Flower (make 3) Using A, make a slip ring (see page 18).
1st round (RS) 3ch, 9dc in ring, pull end to close ring, ss to top ch of 3ch. 10 sts.
2nd round 2ch, 1dc in next dc, 1ch, [dc dec in next 2dc, 1ch] 4 times, ss in top of first dc.
3rd round 4ch, ss in first of 4ch, [ss in 1ch of 2nd round, ss in next dec, 4ch, ss in first of 4ch] 4 times, ss in next ch. Fasten off invisibly (see page 19).
Stem Using B, make 31ch. Skip 1ch, ss in each of next 15ch, [3ch, skip first of 3ch, ss in each of next 2ch, on main stem ss in each of next 7ch] twice, 1sc in last ch. Fasten off invisibly.

Leaf (worked in one round with RS facing)
Using B, make 14ch. Skip 1ch, 1sc in each of next 3ch, 1hdc in next ch, 1dc in each of next 6ch, 1hdc in next ch, 1sc in each of next 2ch, 5ch, skip 3ch, 1sc in next ch, 1ch. Working in the remaining strands of original base ch: 1sc in each of first 2ch, 1hdc in next ch, 1dc in each of next 6ch, 1hdc in next ch, 1sc in each of next 3ch. Working in both strands of each ch: 1sc in next ch, 15ch, skip 1ch, ss in each of next 14ch, 1sc in next ch. Fasten off invisibly.
Making up Sew a flower to the top of the stem and one to each side branch. Join stem and leaf.

STITCH KEY	SEE ALSO
⬭ *Chain*	*Crochet Symbols:* pages 12–13
● *Slip stitch*	*Crochet Abbreviations:* pages 15
+ *Single crochet*	*Notes on Crochet:* pages 18–19
⊤ *Half double crochet*	
⊤ *Double crochet*	
⊤ *Treble crochet*	
⊤ *Double treble crochet*	

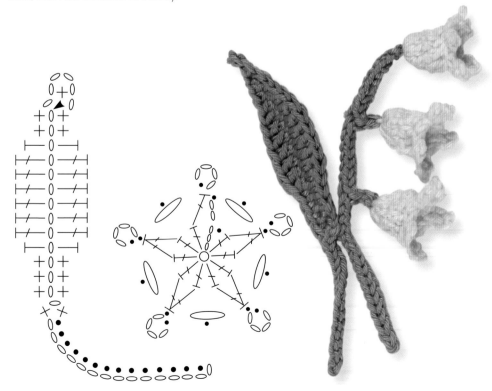

55 SCABIOUS
directory view page 33

Yarn: DK wool in pale blue (A) and deep blue (B)

METHOD

Center Using A, make a slip ring (see page 18).
1st round (RS) 3ch, 15dc in ring, pull end to close ring, ss in top ch of 3ch. 16 sts.
2nd round 4ch, [ss in the front strand of next dc, 3ch] 15 times, ss in first of 4ch. Fasten off invisibly (see page 19).

Petals

3rd round (RS) Working behind 2nd round and into the first round: join B in the top ch of 3ch, 6ch, working in the back strand of each dc: [ss in next dc, 5ch] 15 times, ss in first of 6ch. Fasten off invisibly (see page 19).

56 PERIWINKLE
directory view page 30

Yarn: Fine cotton in pale blue (A), deep blue (B), and pale green (C)

METHOD

Flower Using A, make 4ch, join with ss into a ring.
1st round (RS) 4ch, 4tr in ring, ss to top ch of 4ch. 5 sts.
2nd round 5ch, [1sc in next tr, 4ch] 4 times, ss in first of 5ch. 5 ch loops. Fasten off.
3rd round With center of flower facing, join B in first ch loop, 3ch, 2-st dc cluster around ch loop, 3ch, ss in same loop, [ss, 3ch, 2-st dc cluster, 3ch, ss in next loop] 4 times, ss to first ch. Fasten off invisibly (see page 19).
Stem Using C, make 11ch, skip 1ch, ss in each of next 10ch. Fasten off.
Making up Press petals. Thread one yarn end from the stem through the center of the flower from below. Knot it close to the flower and trim. Use second end to attach stem to base of flower.

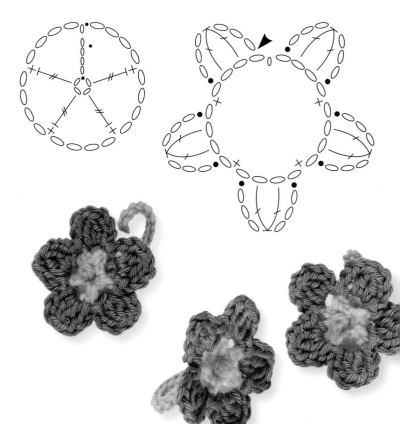

57 GERANIUM
directory view page 28

Yarn: Fine cotton in orange (A), yellow (B), and purple (C)

METHOD

Center Using A, make 5ch, join with ss into a ring.
1st round (RS) 1ch, 7sc in ring, with B ss to 1ch. 8 sts. Continue with B.
2nd round 2ch, 1sc in 1ch below, 2ch, [2sc in next sc, 2ch] 7 times, ss in top ch of 2ch. Fasten off.
3rd round Join C in a ch sp, 2ch, make a popcorn in ch sp below, 2ch, ss in same ch sp, [ss in next ch sp, 2ch, make popcorn, 2ch, ss in same ch sp] 7 times. Fasten off invisibly (see page 19).

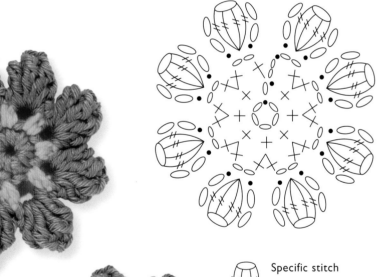

Specific stitch and symbol
Popcorn—4tr; take hook out of loop at top of last tr; insert hook under 2 strands at top of first tr; then in loop, yrh, pull yarn through sts on hook.

58 GRAPES
directory view page 45

Yarn: DK wool in shades of purple (A) and olive (B)

METHOD

Grape (make 19) Using A, make 5ch. Skip 4ch, in next ch make a 6-st tr cluster. Pull yarn tight so that stitches curve with smooth side (RS) to the outside. Make 4ch, from the back ss into ch at base of cluster. Fasten off.
Stem Using B, make 18ch. Skip 1ch, 1sc in each of next 6ch, 5ch, skip 1ch, 1sc in each of next 4ch, 1sc in each of remaining 11ch. Fasten off invisibly (see page 19).
Making up Sew grapes in a formation of 1, 2, 3, 4, 5, 4 as shown in diagram, varying direction of sts. Attach the shortest branch of the stem behind the bunch.

Specific abbreviation and symbol
6-st tr cluster—a cluster made up of 6 trebles: * yrh twice, insert hook and pull loop through, [yrh and pull yarn through 2 loops on hook] twice; repeat from * 5 times, yrh and pull yarn through all 7 loops on hook.

AURICULA
directory view page 28

Yarn: Single strand of embroidery wool or fine wool in lime (A), cream (B), purple (C), and mauve (D)

METHOD

Flower Using A and leaving an end of approximately 2in (5cm), make 4ch, join with ss into a ring.

1st round (RS) 4ch, 6tr in ring, ss to top ch of 4ch. 7 sts. Fasten off invisibly (see page 19).

2nd round With inside of cup facing, join B in a tr, (4ch, 2tr in st below), [1ch, 3tr in next st] 6 times, 1ch, with C ss to top ch of 4ch. 21 sts. Continue with C.

3rd round 3ch, 3dc in next tr; 1dc in next tr, [skip 1ch, 1ch, 1dc in next tr; 3dc in next tr; 1dc in next tr] 6 times, 1ch, with D ss to top ch of 3ch. Continue with D.

4th round 1ch, 2dc in next dc, 2tr in next dc, 2dc in next dc, 1sc in next dc, 1sc around 1ch of 3rd round and 1ch of 2nd round, [1sc in next dc, 2dc in next dc, 2tr in next dc, 2dc in next dc, 1sc in next dc, 1sc around 1ch of 3rd round and 1ch of 2nd round] 6 times, ss to 1ch. Fasten off invisibly.

Stem Using A, make 15ch, skip 1ch, 1sc in each of next 14ch. Fasten off.

Making up Hook first A end into center of flower, knot the end close to the flower and trim. Attach stem.

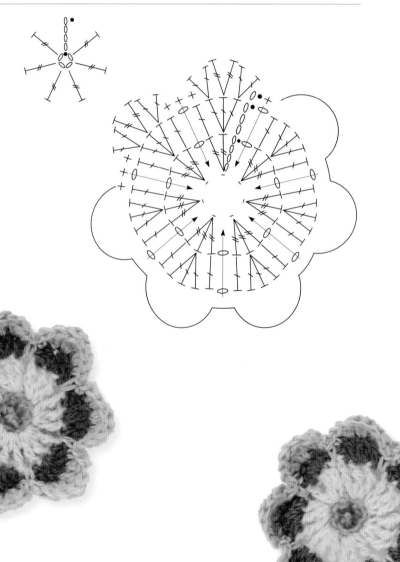

 **Specific symbol**
1sc around 1ch of 3rd round and
1ch of 2nd round.

60 ASTER
directory view page 29

Yarn: Fine cotton in dark green (A), pale green (B), and mauve (C)

METHOD

Flower Leaving a long end, use A to make a slip ring (see page 18).
1st row (RS) 3ch, 4dc in ring, pull end to close ring. 5 sts.
2nd row 3ch, 2dc in each of next 3dc, 1dc in top ch of 3ch. 8 sts.
Fasten off.
3rd row Join B in front strand of top of last dc, [5ch, ss in front strand of next dc] 6 times, 5ch, ss in front strand of top ch of 3ch. 7 loops.
Fasten off invisibly (see page 19).
4th row With RS facing, fold loops forward and join C in back strand of end dc of 2nd row, [8ch, skip 1ch, 1sc in next ch, 1hdc in next ch, 1dc in each of next 3 ch, 1hdc in next ch, 1sc in next ch, ss in back strand of next dc] 7 times, ending ss in back strand of top ch of 3ch of 2nd row.
Fasten off invisibly.
Stem RS facing, insert hook in slip ring at base and pull long end through. Make 10ch, skip 1ch, ss in each of 9ch. Fasten off invisibly.

61 SCOTTISH THISTLE
directory view page 28

Yarn: Fine cotton in gray-green (A) and pale mauve (B)

METHOD

Using A, make 5ch, join with ss into a ring.
1st round (RS) 2ch, 7sc in ring, ss to top ch of 2ch. 8 sts.
2nd round 1ch, [2sc in next sc, 1sc in next sc] 3 times, 2sc in next sc, ss to 1ch. 12 sts.
3rd round 1ch, [2sc in next sc, 1sc in next sc] 5 times, 2sc in next sc, ss to 1ch. 18 sts. Insert a marker and work 3 rounds of sc continuously.
7th round [Dec in next 2 sc, 1sc in next sc] 6 times. 12 sts. Work 2 rounds straight, ending ss in next sc.
10th round * 2ch, ss in first ch, ss in next st; repeat from *, ending ss in first ch. Fasten off invisibly (see page 19).
Top Cut strands of B approximately 5in (13cm) long and enough to fill thistle head when doubled. Fold in half and tie in a tassel. Insert tassel along with a little spare yarn for padding. Secure and trim.
Stem Using A, make 12ch, skip 1ch, ss in next 11ch, turn, 1ch, skip 1ss, ss in single strand of each remaining ss. Fasten off. Sew to base of thistle.

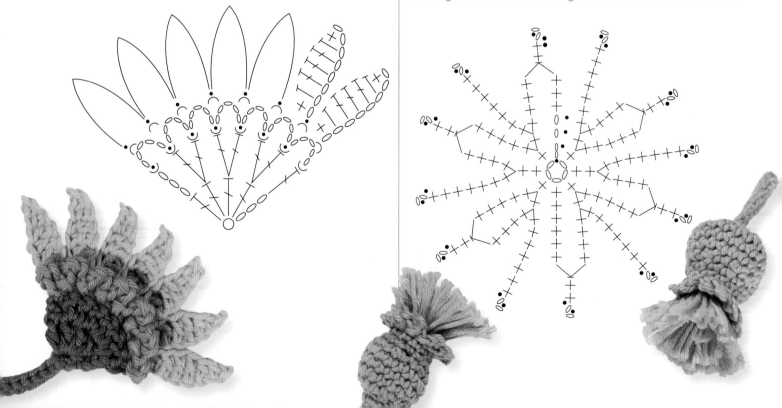

IRISH ROSE

directory view page 23

Yarn: Fine wool in deep pink (A), mid-pink (B), and pale pink (C)

METHOD

1st round (RS) Using A, make a slip ring (see page 18), 2ch, 7sc in ring, pull end to close ring, ss to top ch of 2ch. 8 sts.
2nd round 2ch, 1sc in base of first ch, 2sc in each of next 7 sts, ss to top ch of 2ch. 16 sts.
3rd round 4ch, [skip 1sc, 1sc in next sc, 3ch] 7 times, ss to first ch of 4ch. 8ch sp.
4th round [1sc, 1hdc, 1dc, 1hdc, 1sc] in each ch sp. 8 petals. Fasten off with B. Continue with B.
5th round Folding petals forward and working into the back of petals, ss in the 2 strands that form the base of each of first 3 sts of next petal, [3ch, 1sc in base of dc at center of next petal] 7 times, 3ch, ss in 3rd of 3ss.
6th round [1sc, 1hdc, 3dc, 1hdc, 1sc] in each ch sp. Fasten off with C. Continue with C.
7th round Folding petals forward and working into the back of petals as before, ss in base of each of next 4 sts, [5ch, 1sc in base of center dc] 7 times, 5ch, ss in 4th of 4ss.
8th round [1sc, 1hdc, 5dc, 1hdc, 1sc] in each ch sp. Fasten off.

Specific symbols

• ss in the base at the back of the st below.

+ sc in the base at the back of the st below.

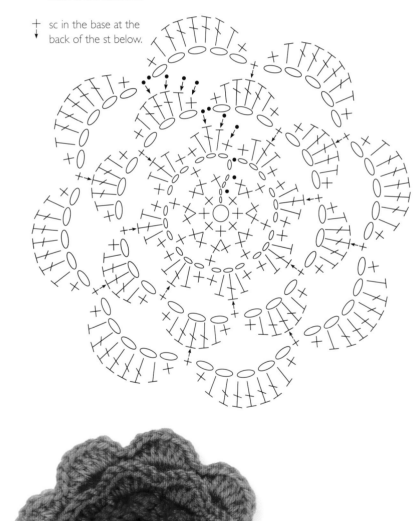

63 ROLLED ROSE AND ROSEBUDS
directory view page 25

Yarn: Embroidery cotton in pale pink (A), mid-pink (B), deep pink (C), and green (D)

METHOD

Rose

Picot row Using A, make 5ch, skip 4ch, 1sc in next ch, [8ch, skip 4ch, 1sc in next ch] 6 times, turn. 7 picots.

1st row (WS) 1ch, 7sc in first picot sp, [1ss over 3ch, 7sc in next picot] 6 times. Fasten off. Do not turn, join B in first ch.

2nd row 1ch, [1sc in each of 2sc, 2hdc in each of next 3sc, 1sc in each of next 2sc, ss over 3ch between picots] 5 times. Fasten off. Do not turn, join C in first ch.

3rd row 1ch, [1sc in each of 2sc, 1hdc in next hdc, 1dc in each of next 4hdc, 1hdc in next hdc, 1sc in each of next 2sc, ss over 3ch between picots] 3 times. Fasten off.

With smallest petals at center, roll and stitch.

Stem Leaving an end approximately 4in (10cm) long, join D at base of rose. Weaving end across between each ch, make 11ch. Skip 1ch, 1sc in each of next 10ch. Fasten off.

Sepals Make 5ch, wrap ch around stem and ss in first ch.

1st round 1ch, 9sc in 5ch sp, ss in first sc. 9 sts.

2nd round 1ch, 1sc in each sc, ss in first sc.

3rd round 1ch, [2sc in first sc, 1sc in each of next 2sc] 3 times, ss in first sc. 12 sts. Fasten off, leaving an end to stitch sepals to base of rose.

Rosebud (make 3) Using A work picot row as for rose until 6 picots have been completed, turn. Work 1st row, repeating instructions in brackets 5 times. Fasten off.

Noting that first row is RS, roll and stitch to form rosebuds.

Stem Using D, make 12ch, ss in base of first rosebud, turn and ss in each of 4ch, make 4ch, ss in base of 2nd rosebud, turn and ss in each of 4ch, make 4ch, ss in base of 3rd rosebud, turn and ss in each of 4ch and first 8ch. Fasten off.

Sepals Holding rosebud in left hand, wrap yarn once around finger and base of rosebud to form a ring.

1st round 1ch, 6sc in ring, pull end to close ring, ss in first sc.

2nd round 1ch, 2sc in each sc, ss in first sc. Fasten off. Finish 2nd and 3rd rosebuds in same way. Stitch sepals to base of rosebuds.

64 WILD ROSE
directory view page 24

Yarn: DK wool in yellow (A), white (B), and pink (C)

METHOD

Center Using A, make a slip ring (see page 18).
1st round (RS) 2ch, 9sc in ring, pull end to close ring, using B ss in top ch of 2ch. 10 sts. Continue with B.
2nd round 1ch, [2sc in next sc, 1sc in next sc] 4 times, 2sc in next sc, using C ss in 1ch. 15 sts. Fasten off. Continue with C.
First petal
1st row (RS) 1ch, 1sc in each of next 2sc. 3 sts.
2nd row 1ch, 1sc in next sc, 1sc in 1ch.
3rd row 4ch, (1dtr, 1tr) in sc below, 1dc in next sc, (1tr, 1dtr, 1tr) in 1ch. 7 sts. Fasten off invisibly (see page 19).
2nd petal (RS) Join C in next sc of 2nd round and then work as first petal. Make 3 more petals as the 2nd petal.
Stamens Cut 4 lengths of A, each approximately 4¾in (12cm) long. Thread one on a wool needle, leaving an end long enough to knot, take it through the edge of the center ring, make a backstitch on the WS and bring it to the front. Do the same with remaining lengths of A, then knot them and trim them.

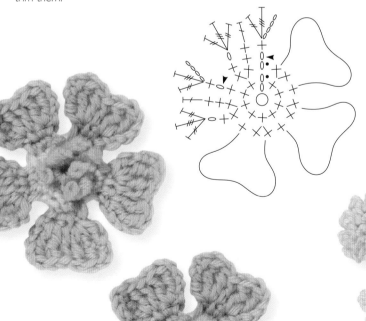

65 OLD-FASHIONED PINK
directory view page 26

Yarn: Fine cotton in pink (A), magenta (B), and white (C)

METHOD

Center Using A, make a slip ring, (see page 18).
1st round (RS) 3ch, 9dc in ring, pull end to close ring, with B ss in top ch of 3ch. 10 sts. Continue with B.
2nd round 1ch, 1sc in st below, 2sc in each of next 9dc, with C ss in 1ch. 20 sts. Continue with C.
First petal
1st row (RS) 4ch, 2tr in each of next 3sc, turn.
2nd row 1ch, 1sc in each of next 5tr.
3rd row [4ch, ss in next sc] 4 times, 4ch, ss in 1ch, do not turn, 4ch, ss in next sc of 2nd round. Without fastening off, work 4 more petals in this way, ending ss in first ch of first petal. Fasten off invisibly (see page 19).

RADISHES

directory view page 45

Yarn: Stranded embroidery wool or fine wool in white (A), pale pink (B), deep pink (C), and 2 shades of green (D)
Extras: Batting

METHOD

Radish Using A and leaving an end of approximately 2in (5cm), make 6ch, skip 3ch, ss in next ch.

1st round (RS) 2ch, 5sc in ring, ss in top ch of 2ch. 6 sts.

2nd round 2ch, 1sc in st below, 2sc in each sc, with B ss in top ch of 2ch. 12 sts. Continue with B.

3rd round 1sc in each st.

4th round [2sc in next sc, 1sc in next sc] 6 times. 18 sts. Change to C.

5th–8th rounds 1sc in each sc.

9th round [1 dec in next 2sc] 9 times. 9 sts. Hook first end to RS, then insert batting into cavity.

10th round 1sc in next st, [1 dec in next 2 sts] 4 times. 5 sts. Fasten off.

Leaf (make 3 for each radish) Using D, make 9ch, skip 1ch, 1sc in each of next 8ch, 1ch, working in remaining strand of ch, 1sc in each of next 6ch, turn, 1ch, 1sc in each of next 5sc, 3sc in 1ch sp, 1sc in each of next 6sc. Fasten off. Attach leaf to radish.

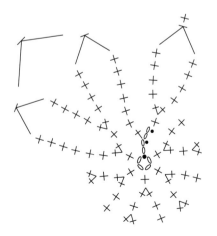

67 APPLE BLOSSOM
directory view page 25

Yarn: DK wool in lime (A) and pink (B)

METHOD

Center Using A, make a slip ring (see page 18).
1st round (RS) 2ch, 9sc in ring, pull end to close ring, using B ss in top ch of 2ch. 10 sts. Continue with B.
Petals
2nd round 1ch, * (1tr, 2dtr, 1tr) in next sc, ss in next sc; repeat from * 3 times more, (1tr, 2dtr, 1tr) in next sc, ss in 1ch. 5 petals.
Fasten off invisibly (see page 19).

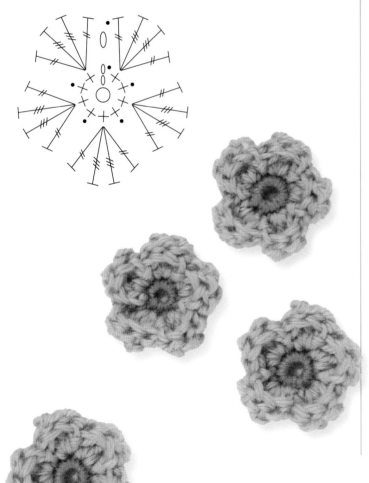

68 PELARGONIUM
directory view page 23

Yarn: Fine cotton in pink (A) and green (B)

METHOD

Flower (make 5)
Petals (RS) Using A, [6ch, skip 5ch, 3dtr in next ch, 5ch, ss in first of 6ch] 5 times, join into a ring with ss in first ch. Fasten off invisibly (see page 19).
Center RS facing and holding yarn underneath, join B by pulling a loop through the base of one petal, ss in the base of each of next 4 petals, ss in join. Leaving a long end of approximately 8in (20cm), fasten off invisibly. Thread this end on to a wool needle and take through the center to the WS. Fasten off all ends except this one.
Stem Knot the 5 long ends close to the flowers. Starting at the knot, use one end to work 16sc over the other 4 ends. Fasten off invisibly. One at a time, thread an end on to a fine wool needle, take it over a sc and then through the stem to the flower, work 2 or 3sc above the knot to secure the flower. Fasten off.

69   RED ADMIRAL BUTTERFLY
directory view page 32, 39

Yarn: DK wool in khaki (A), orange (B), and black (C)

METHOD

First pair of wings Using A, make 5ch, join with ss into a ring.
1st row (WS) 3ch, 4dc in ring. 5 sts.
2nd row 3ch, 2dc in each of next 3dc, working last wrap with B 1dc in top ch of 3ch. 8 sts. Continue with B.
3rd row 1ch, 1hdc in next dc, 3dc in next dc, 1hdc in each of next 2dc, 3dc in next dc, 1hdc in next dc, working last wrap with C 1sc in top ch of 3ch. 12 sts. Continue with C.
4th row 1ch, 1sc in hdc, 2sc in each of next 2dc, 1sc in next dc, ss under 3 strands of next hdc, 1sc in next hdc, 2sc in next dc, (1dc, 1tr, 1dc) in next dc, 1dc in next dc, 1sc in hdc, ss in 1ch. Fasten off invisibly (see page 19).
2nd pair of wings With WS facing, join A in 5ch ring and work 1st to 3rd rows as first pair of wings.
4th row 1ch, 1sc in hdc, 1dc in next dc, (1dc, 1tr, 1dc) in next dc, 2sc in next dc, 1sc in next hdc, ss under 3 strands of next hdc, 1sc in next dc, 2sc in each of next 2dc, 1sc in hdc, ss in ch. Fasten off invisibly.
Body Using A, make 10ch, skip 2ch, 1sc in next ch, 1ch, ss in each of remaining 7ch. Fasten off.
Making up Join wings in center and stitch body over join.

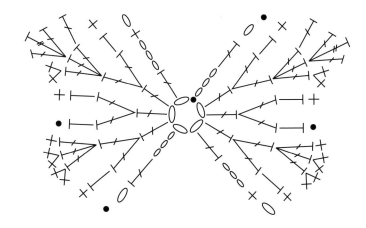

70 BUMBLEBEE

directory view page 34

Yarn: DK wool in black (A), yellow (B), and white (C)

METHOD

Body Using A, make a slip ring (see page 18).
1st round (RS) 3ch, 7dc in ring, pull end to close ring, with B ss to top ch of 3ch. 8 sts. Continue with B.
2nd round 2ch, [2sc in next dc, 1sc in next dc] 3 times, 2sc in next dc, with A ss to top ch of 2ch. 12 sts. Continue with A.
3rd round 2ch, 1sc in each of next 11sc, with B ss to top ch of 2ch. Continue with B.
4th round As 3rd round, working ss with A. Continue with A.
5th round 1ch, [tr dec in next 2sc, 1sc in next sc] 3 times, tr dec in next 2sc, ss to 1ch. 8 sts. Fasten off invisibly (see page 19).
Wings Using C, [make 6ch, skip 5ch, 2-st dtr cluster in next ch, 5ch, ss in same ch as cluster] twice. Fasten off invisibly.
Making up Use yarn to fill body. With color joins underneath, flatten the body a little and with A join the two sides of the opening for the head. Attach wings with A.

71 NARCISSUS

directory view page 38

Yarn: DK cotton in pale green (A), orange (B), and yellow (C)

METHOD

Center Using A, make 4ch, join with ss into a ring.
1st round (RS) 1ch, 5sc in ring, using B ss to 1ch. 6 sts. Continue with B.
2nd round 3ch, working in the front strand of each st: 1dc in ss below, 2dc in each of next 5 sc, ss in 3rd of 3ch. 12 sts. Fasten off invisibly (see page 19).
Petals Place left thumb inside the center and RS facing, work in the back strand of each st of the first round: join C in a sc of first round, [6ch, skip 1ch, 1sc in next ch, 1hdc in next ch, 1dc in next ch, 1tr in next ch, 1dtr in next ch, ss in next st of first round] 6 times, ending ss in same st as join. Fasten off.

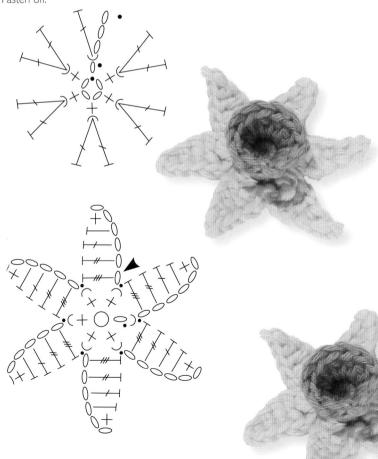

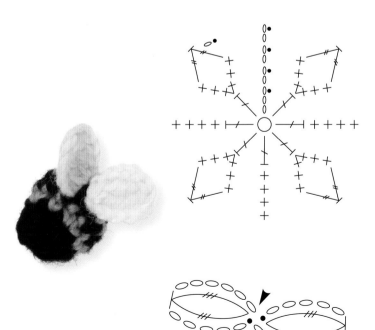

72 SANTOLINA
directory view page 39

Yarn: DK cotton in yellow (A) and green (B)

METHOD

Flower Using A, make a slip ring (see page 18).
Working in a round with RS facing, make 5 ch, into ring work 2-st dtr cluster 7 times, pull end to close ring, skip 5ch and ss in top of first cluster. Fasten off leaving an end long enough to gather top of clusters.
Stem Using B, make 12ch, skip 1ch, ss in each of next 5ch, 10ch, skip 1ch, ss in each of next 4ch, 8ch, skip 1ch, ss in each of next 7ch, 1ch, ss in each of next 5ch, 1ch, ss in each of remaining 6ch.
Fasten off invisibly (see page 19).
Making up The long clusters will have curled to the back naturally, so use the yarn end to gather them a little more and secure them. Attach a stem.

73 HELENIUM
directory view page 38

Yarn: DK wool in orange (A), yellow (B), and lemon (C)

METHOD

Center Using A, make a slip ring (see page 18).
1st round (RS) 2ch, 7sc in ring, pull end to close ring, ss in top ch of 2ch. 8 sts.
2nd round 1ch, 2sc in next sc, [1sc in next sc, 2sc in next sc] 3 times, with B ss in 1ch. 12 sts. Continue with B.
3rd round [4ch, ss in front strand of next sc] 12 times, ending ss in ss of previous round. 12 loops. Fasten off invisibly (see page 19).
4th round Join C in the back strand of first sc in 2nd round, [10ch, 1sc in back strand of next st] 12 times, ending ss in first ch. 12 loops. Fasten off invisibly.

✛ **Specific symbol**
sc in back strand of sc of 2nd round.

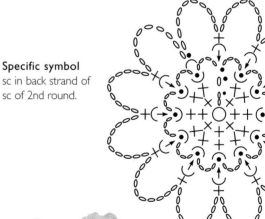

CAMOMILE
directory view page 40

Yarn: Fine wool in yellow (A), green (B), and white (C)

METHOD

Center Using A, make a slip ring (see page 18).
1st round (RS) 2ch, 5sc in ring, pull end to close ring, ss in top ch of 2ch. 6 sts.
2nd round 1ch, 1sc in st below, 2sc in each of next 5sc, ss in 1ch. 12 sts.
3rd round 1ch, [2sc in next sc, 1sc in next sc] 5 times, 2sc in next sc, ss in 1ch. 18 sts.
4th round 1ch, [2sc in next sc, 1sc in each of next 2sc] 5 times, 2sc in next sc, 1sc in next sc, with B ss in 1ch. 24 sts. Continue with B.
5th round 1ch, [2sc in next sc, 1sc in each of next 3sc] 5 times, 2sc in next sc, 1sc in each of next 2sc, with C ss in 1ch. Do not break yarn B. 30 sts.
6th round Using C, 3ch, [1dc in each of next 2sc, 7ch, skip 1sc] 9 times, 2dc in each of next 2sc, 3ch, ss in first ch of 3ch. Fasten off.
7th round Using B, insert hook in st below join and make a sc over this, [3ch, folding petal forward, insert hook in empty sc of previous round, pull yarn through then take hook over 7ch to make a sc enclosing 7ch] 9 times, 3ch, ss in first sc. Fasten off.

 Specific symbol
sc worked over ch and into sc
of previous round.

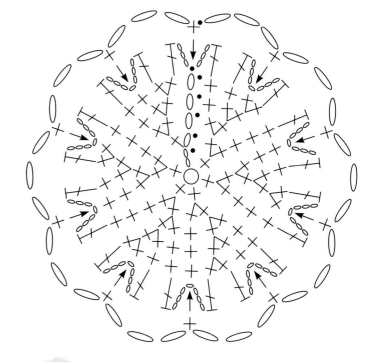

75   ZINNIA
directory view page 37

Yarn: DK wool in yellow (A) and lime (B)

METHOD

Petals (RS) Using A, [make 7ch, skip 3ch, 5dc in next ch, skip 2ch, ss in next ch] 9 times. 9 petals. Fasten off.

Joining row RS facing, place petals flat, straight edges uppermost, and join A with a sc in 4th ch of first petal, working behind petals, [1ch, 1sc in 4th ch of next petal] 8 times, 1ch, ss to first sc. Fasten off.

Center Using B, make 5ch, join with ss into ring. Working over yarn end for additional padding, 1ch, 9sc in ring, ss to 1ch. Fasten off invisibly (see page 19), leaving an end to sew with.

Making up Darn in ends of petals. Turn center to WS and using backstitch over edge chain, stitch to center of flower.

76   IRISH LEAF
directory view page 23, 36, 42

Yarn: DK wool

METHOD

Make 12ch.

1st row (WS) Skip 1ch, 1sc in each of next 10ch, 5sc in next ch, without turning over and working in the remaining strand of base ch: 1sc in each of next 10ch, 3ch, working under both strands of each st: 1sc in each of next 9sc, turn.

2nd row 1ch, working in back strand only: 1sc in each of next 8sc, [1sc in back strand of next ch, 1ch] twice, 1sc in next ch, 1sc in each of next 9sc, turn.

3rd row 1ch, skip 1sc, working under both strands: 1sc in each of next 9sc, [1ch, 1sc in next st] 4 times, 1sc in each of next 6sc, turn.

4th row 1ch, skip 1sc, working in back strand only: 1sc in each of next 20 sts, turn.

5th row 1ch, skip 1sc, working in both strands: 1sc in each of next 9 sts, **stem:** 7ch, skip 1ch, ss in each of next 6ch, ss in last sc of 5th row. Fasten off invisibly (see page 19).

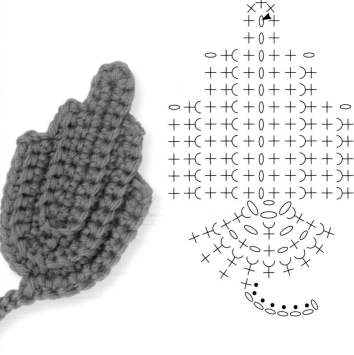

77   OAK LEAF
directory view page 42

Yarn: DK wool in rust (A) and olive (B)

METHOD

1st row (RS) Using A, make 10ch, skip 1ch, ss in each of next 9ch; 7ch, skip 3ch, 1dc in each of next 2ch, 1sc in each of next 2ch; 9ch, skip 3ch, 1dc in each of next 2ch, 1sc in next ch; 8ch, skip 3ch, 1dc in next ch, 1sc in next ch; 6ch, skip 3ch, 1dc in next ch; 1sc in each of next 2ch; 5ch, skip 3ch, 1dc in next ch, 1sc in next ch; 1sc in each of 3ch stem; 6ch, skip 3ch, 1dc in each of next 2ch, 1sc in next ch, 1sc in each of 3ch stem; 7ch, skip 3ch, 1dc in each of next 2ch, 1sc in each of next 2ch, ss in top ch of stem. Fasten off.

2nd row (RS) Working in single remaining strand of ch at base of sts from now on: join B in first ch of first 7ch, 1ch, 1sc in each of next 3 sts; working into 2 strands of 3 free ch and tops of sts from now on: 1sc in first ch, 2sc in 2nd ch, 1sc in 3rd ch, 1sc in each of next 3 sts; 1sc in center ch of stem, 1sc in each of next 3 sts, (1sc, 2sc, 1sc) in 3ch, 1sc in each of next 3 sts, 1sc in center ch of stem, 1sc in each of next 2 sts, (1sc, 2sc, 1sc) in 3ch, 1sc in next st, skip 1ch of stem, 1sc in each of next 2ch, (1sc, 2sc, 1sc) in 3ch, 1sc in each of next 5 sts, (1sc, 2sc, 1sc) in 3ch, 1sc in each of the next 2 sts, skip 1sc, 1sc in next sc, skip next sc, 1sc in each of next 3 sts, (1sc, 2sc, 1sc) in 3ch, 1sc in each of next 3 sts, skip 1sc, 1sc in next sc, skip next sc, 1sc in each of next 4 sts, (1sc, 2sc, 1sc) in 3ch, 1sc in each of next 3 sts, ss in next st. Fasten off invisibly (see page 19).

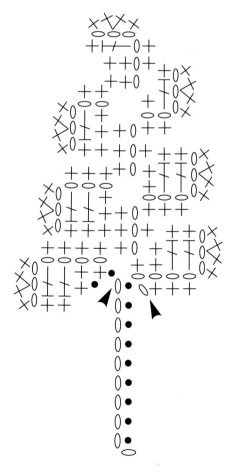

78 GINKGO LEAF

directory view page 42

Yarn: DK wool

METHOD

Leaf Make 11ch.

1st row (RS) Skip 1ch, 1sc in each of next 4ch, 1hdc in next ch, 1dc in each of next 5ch. 11 sts. From now on, work in the back strand of each st:

2nd row 3ch, 1dc in each of next 4dc, 1hdc in 1hdc, 1sc in each of next 4sc, 1sc in 1ch.

3rd row 1ch, 1sc in each of next 4sc, 1hdc in 1hdc, 1dc in each of next 4dc, 1dc in top ch of 3ch.

4th row As 2nd row.

5th row 1ch, 1sc in each of next 4sc, 1hdc in 1hdc, 1dc in each of next 3dc, turn.

6th row 4ch, skip 3ch, 1dc in next ch, 1dc in each of next 3dc, 1hdc in 1hdc, 1sc in each of next 4sc, 1sc in 1ch.

7th row As 3rd row.

8th row As 2nd row.

9th row As 3rd row. Fasten off invisibly (see page 19).

Base Turn to RS. Working under 2 strands, join yarn in 1ch at beginning of first row, 2ch, 4-st dc cluster in 1ch of 3rd, 5th, 7th, and 9th rows. Do not fasten off.

Stem Make 10ch, skip 1ch, 1sc in each of next 9ch. Fasten off.

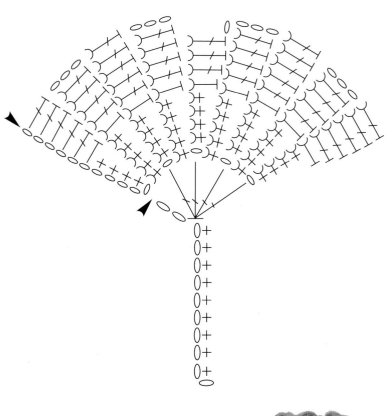

79 IVY LEAF
directory view page 43

Yarn: Fine wool in dark green (A) and pale green (B)

METHOD

Stem Using A, make 12ch, skip 2ch, 1sc in next ch, ss in each of next 9ch. Do not fasten off.
Leaf
1st row (RS) [5ch, skip 4ch, 1sc in next ch] 3 times, ss in remaining strand of top ch of stem, turn. 3 ch loops.
2nd row In first loop: (2sc, 1ch, 1dc, 1ch, 2sc); in 2nd loop: (1sc, 1dc, 1ch, [1tr, 1ch] twice, 1dc, 1sc); in 3rd loop: (2sc, 1ch, 1dc, 1ch, 2sc), turn. Fasten off.
3rd row Join B in last sc of 2nd row; *first lobe*: 1ch, 2sc in next sc, 2sc in 1ch, 1ch, 1dc in dc, 1ch, 2sc in 1ch, 2sc in next sc, ss in next sc; *2nd lobe*: 1sc in sc, (1sc, 1dc) in dc, 2dc in 1ch, 1ch, (2tr, 1ch, 1dtr) in tr; skip 1ch, 2dc in next tr; 1dc in 1ch, (1dc, 1sc) in next dc, ss in 1sc; *3rd lobe*: 1sc in sc, 2sc in next sc, 2sc in 1ch, 1ch, 1dc in dc, 1ch, 2sc in 1ch, 2sc in sc, 1sc in next sc. Fasten off invisibly (see page 19).

80 FERN LEAF
directory view page 22, 33, 43

Yarn: DK cotton

METHOD

First leaf Make 12ch, * skip 1ch, 1sc in next ch, 1hdc in next ch, 1dc in next ch, 1tr in next ch, 1dc in next ch, 1hdc in next ch, 1sc in next ch. **
2nd leaf Make 12ch, * skip 1ch, 1sc in next ch, 1hdc in next ch, 1dc in next ch, 1tr in each of next 2ch, 1dc in next ch, 1hdc in next ch, 1sc in next ch. **
3rd leaf As 2nd leaf.
4th leaf Make 11ch, then work as first leaf from * to **.
5th leaf Make 8ch, then work as first leaf from * to **.
6th leaf As 5th leaf.
Stem Ss in each of next 3ch.
7th leaf Make 9ch, then work as 2nd leaf from * to **.
Stem Ss in each of next 3ch.
8th leaf As 7th leaf.
Stem Ss in each of next 3ch.
9th leaf As 5th leaf.
Stem Ss in each of next 4 ch.
Fasten off invisibly (see page 19).

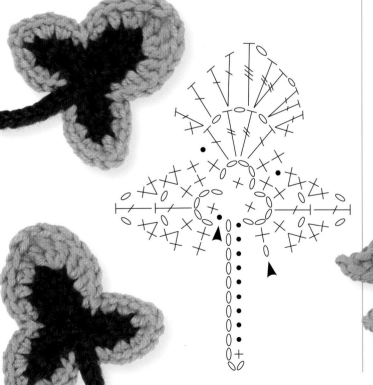

ADVANCED DESIGNS

MARIGOLD
directory view page 37

Yarn: Fine cotton in orange (A) and green (B)

METHOD

Using A, make a slip ring (see page 18).
1st round (RS) 2ch, 9sc in ring, pull end to close ring, ss to top ch of 2ch. 10 sts.
2nd round [5ch, skip 1ch, ss in each of next 4ch, ss in front strand only of next st] 10 times. 10 petals.
3rd round Bending petals forward in order to work into the remaining strand of each st of first round, ss in first st, 2ch, 1sc in each of next 9 sts, ss in top ch of 2ch. 10 sts.
4th round [5ch, skip 1ch, ss in each of next 4ch, ss in front strand only of st below, 5ch, skip 4ch, ss in each of next 4ch, ss in front strand of the next st] 10 times. 20 petals.

5th round Bending petals forward in order to work into the remaining strand of each st of 3rd round, ss in first st, then work as 4th round, ending ss in first ss. 20 petals. Fasten off.
Stem and sepals Using B, make 11ch, skip 1ch, ss in each of next 10ch, 3ch, 7dc in remaining strand of top ch of stem, ss in top ch of 3ch, turn to work around inside of cup: [2ch, skip 1ch, ss in next ch, ss in next st] 8 times. Fasten off invisibly (see page 19).
Making up With A, make a small tassel and string it with B. Thread B on to a wool needle, take it through the center of the flower and use it to secure the sepals and stem. Trim tassel.

STITCH KEY

⌒	Chain
●	Slip stitch
+	Single crochet
│	Half double crochet
⊤	Double crochet
⊤	Treble crochet
⫲	Double treble crochet

SEE ALSO

Crochet Symbols: pages 12–13

Crochet Abbreviations: page 15

Notes on Crochet: pages 18–19

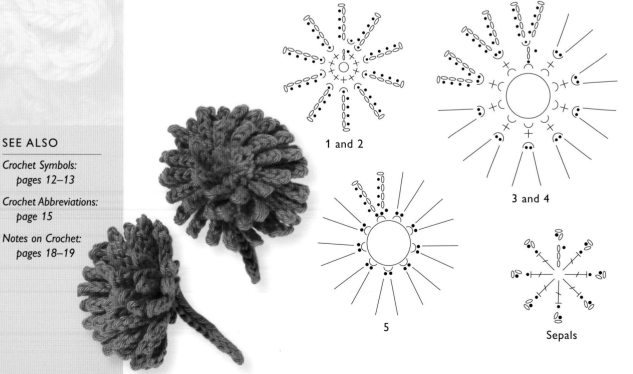

1 and 2

3 and 4

5

Sepals

82 GERBERA
directory view page 36

Yarn: DK wool in yellow (A), orange (B), and green (C)

METHOD

Center Using A, make a slip ring (see page 18).
1st round (RS) 1ch, 12sc in ring, remove hook, insert from back in first sc, catch loop and pull through, pull end to close ring.
2nd round 1ch, 1sc around the stem of each sc, remove hook, insert from back in first sc, catch loop and pull through. Fasten off invisibly (see page 19).
First round of petals Join B in a sc of 2nd round of center.
1st petal Make 8ch loosely, working into the back loop only of each ch each time, skip 1ch, ss in next ch, 1sc in each of next 2ch, 1hdc in each of next 4ch, remove hook, insert from back in same sc of 2nd round, catch loop and pull through.
2nd–12th petals Remove hook, insert from front in next sc of 2nd round, catch loop and pull through, then work as 1st petal.

2nd round of petals
Next round Working behind first round of petals, remove hook, insert from front in strand at base of 1st petal, catch loop and pull through, 1ch, 1sc in same strand, [1ch, 1sc in strand between next 2 petals] 11 times, remove hook, insert in front of first sc, catch loop and pull through.
Petals Work one petal in each sc of previous round as petals of first round.
Stem Join C in a strand between petals of 2nd round.
1st round Working behind petals, 1ch, 1sc in same place as join, [1sc in 2 strands between next 2 petals] 11 times, ss in first sc. 12 sts.
2nd round 1ch, 1sc in each sc, ss in first sc.
3rd round 1ch, [1 dec in next 2sc, 1sc in next sc] 4 times, ss in first st. 8 sts.
4th round 1ch, [1 dec in next 2 sts] 4 times. 4 sts.
Work 5 rounds sc. Fasten off.

Specific symbol
⟂ 1sc around the stem (from the back) of the stitch indicated.

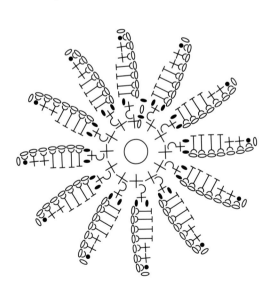

DAFFODIL
directory view page 38

Yarn: DK cotton

METHOD

Petals

1st ring (RS) Make 12ch, join with ss into a ring. 5ch, 2-st dtr dec in next 2ch of ring, 2ch, skip 1ch, ss in next ch, 5ch, ss in next ch of ring, [ss in next ch, 5ch, 2-st dtr dec in next 2ch, 2ch, skip 1ch, ss in next ch, 5ch, ss in next ch] twice. Fasten off invisibly (see page 19).
3 petals.

2nd ring As first ring.

Trumpet Join rings: RS uppermost, place one ring of petals on top of the other, the top petals lying at an angle to those below. Holding the yarn underneath and using a smaller size hook, insert the hook from the top in a remaining single strand of a ch in the top ring and in the remaining strand of the ch in the ring immediately below, yrh, pull loop through both ch, inserting hook in center sp, catch yarn and pull it through 2 loops on hook to make a sc. Work into each pair of ch in this way until 12sc have been completed. Leave loop. Cut yarn to approximately 4½yd (4m) length and pull this through center ring in order to work into the sc just made.

1st round (RS) 1ch, 1sc in each of next 11sc, ss in 1ch.

2nd round 3ch, 1dc in each of next 11sc, ss in top ch of 3ch.

3rd round [2ch, skip 1ch, ss in next ch, ss in next dc] 12 times, ending ss in first ch. Fasten off invisibly.

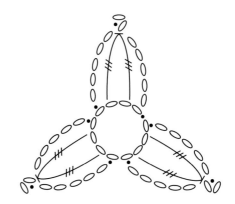

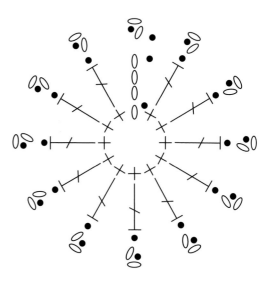

84   ORANGE-TIP BUTTERFLY

directory view page 24, 28

Yarn: DK wool in white (A), pale orange (B), and black (C)

METHOD

Note: The butterfly is worked in rows, but these are all right side rows.
Both pairs of wings Using A, make 15ch.
1st row (RS) Skip 5ch, 3dtr in next ch, 1ch, 1dc in next ch, 2ch, 2dtr in next ch, 1tr in next ch, 3ch, ss in next ch, 3ch, 1tr in next ch, 2dtr in next ch, 1 ch, 1dc in next ch, 2ch, 3dtr in next ch, 5ch, ss in next ch. Fasten off.
2nd row (RS) Using B, join yarn in 2nd ch of 2nd wing, 1ch, (1sc, 1dc) in next st, (1dc, 1ch, 1tr, 1dc) in next st, (1dc, 1sc) in next st, 1ch, ss in top ch of 3ch. Fasten off invisibly (see page 19).
3rd row (RS) Using B, join yarn in 3rd ch of 3rd wing, 1ch, (1sc, 1dc) in next st, (1dc, 1tr, 1ch, 1dc) in next st, (1dc, 1sc) in next st, 1ch, ss in 1ch. Fasten off invisibly.
4th row (RS) Using C, join yarn in 2nd dc of 2nd wing tip, 1ch, (1sc, 1ch, 1sc) in tr, 1ch, ss in dc. Fasten off invisibly.
5th row (RS) Using C, join yarn in 2nd dc of 3rd wing tip, 1ch, (1sc, 1ch, 1sc) in tr, 1ch, ss in next dc. Fasten off invisibly.
Body With C, make 6ch, skip 1ch, 2sc in next ch. Fasten off invisibly.
Making up Gathering up slightly, join wings in center. Sew body in place, leaving 2 ends of C for antennae; split the yarn and cut away excess strands. With C, embroider a spot on each upper wing.

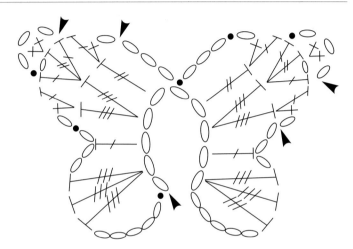

85 SUNFLOWER
directory view page 37

Yarn: Fine wool in dark olive (A) and yellow (B)

METHOD

Center Using A, make a slip ring (see page 18).
1st round (RS) 2ch, 7sc in ring, pull end to close ring, ss in top ch of 2ch.
8 sts.
2nd round 3ch, * (1 popcorn, 1ch, 1sc, 1ch) in next sc; repeat from *
6 times, 1 popcorn in ss of previous round, 1ch, ss in 2nd of 3ch.
8 popcorns and 8 sts.
3rd round 2ch, 2sc in ch below, [3sc in next sc] 7 times, ss in 2nd of 2ch.
24 sts.
4th round 3ch, [1 popcorn in next sc, 1ch, 1sc in next sc, 1ch] 11 times,
1 popcorn in next sc, 1ch, ss in 2nd of 3ch. 12 popcorns and 12 sts.
5th round 2ch, 2sc in same ch below, [3sc in next sc] 11 times, ss in 2nd
ch of 2ch. 36 sts.
6th round 3ch, [1 popcorn in next sc, 1ch, 1sc in next sc, 1ch] 17 times,
1 popcorn in next sc, 1ch, ss in 2nd of 3ch. 18 popcorns and 18 sts.
Fasten off.
Petals
7th round (RS) Join B in a sc, [4ch, skip 1ch, 1sc in next ch, 1hdc in
next ch, 1dc in next ch, ss in next sc of 6th round] 18 times. Fasten
off invisibly (see page 19).

ⱺ **Specific stitch and symbol**
Popcorn—3dc in next st, withdraw
hook leaving loop free, insert
hook in the top of first dc,
then in free loop, yrh
and pull yarn
through both.

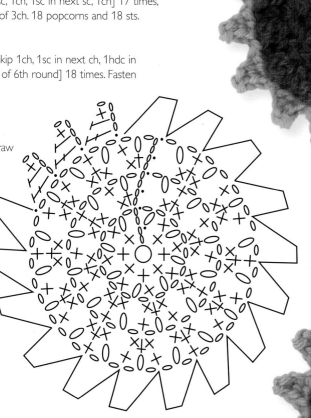

86	## ACORN *directory view page 42*

Yarn: DK wool in dark olive (A) and light olive (B)

METHOD

Acorn Using A, make 5ch, join with ss into a ring.
1st round (RS) 1ch, 7sc in ring, ss in 1ch. 8 sts.
2nd round 1ch, [2sc in next sc, 1sc in next sc] 3 times, 2sc in next sc, ss in 1ch. 12 sts.
3rd round 1ch, 1sc in each sc, ss in 1ch. Fasten off invisibly (see page 19). Allow the cup shape to curl so that the WS of the sts is facing.
4th round Now working in the opposite direction to the previous round and inserting the hook in the single back strand of each st: join B, 4ch, 3-st dtr dec in next 3 sts, [4-st dtr dec in next 4 sts] twice, ss in top ch of 4ch. Fasten off.
Gather the top, stuffing the acorn with B yarn.
Stem Using A, make 11ch, skip 1ch, ss in each of next 10ch. Fasten off invisibly. Attach to base of acorn.

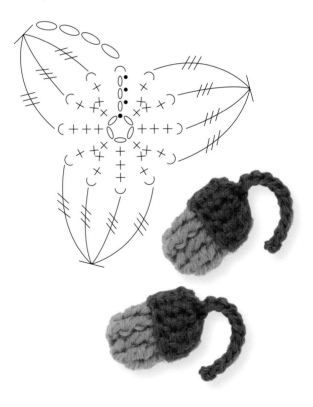

87	## TULIP TREE LEAF *directory view page 43*

Yarn: DK wool

METHOD

Make 10ch.
1st row (RS) Skip 2ch, 1sc in each of next 8ch, 5ch, ss in first of 5ch, 2ch, working in remaining strand of base ch: 1sc in each of next 8ch, 1sc in top ch of 2ch, 3ch; working in back strand only from now on: 1sc in 1ch, 1sc in each of next 3sc, 1hdc in next sc, 1dc in each of next 4sc, turn.
2nd row 3ch, 1dc in each of next 3dc, 1hdc in hdc, 1sc in each of next 4sc, 5sc in 3ch sp, 1sc in each of next 4sc, 1hdc in next sc, 1dc in each of next 4 sts, turn.
3rd row 3ch, 1dc in each of next 3dc, 1hdc in hdc, 1sc in each of next 6sc, 3ch, skip 1sc, 1sc in each of next 6sc, 1hdc in hdc, 1dc in each of next 4 sts, turn.
4th row 3ch, 1dc in each of next 3dc, 1hdc in hdc, 1sc in each of next 6sc, 5sc in ch sp, 1sc in each of next 6sc, 1 hdc in hdc, 1dc in each of next 4 sts. Fasten off invisibly (see page 19).
Stem Turn leaf to WS, join yarn in back of center sc of base, 9ch, skip 1ch, 1sc in each of next 8ch, ss in base of leaf. Fasten off.

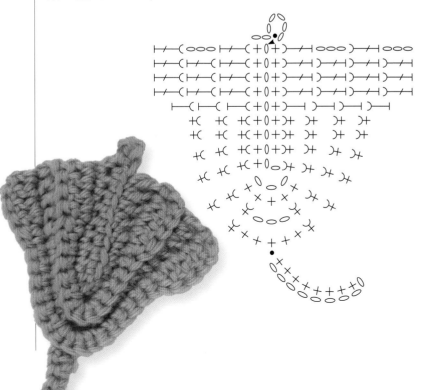

88   PEAPOD
directory view page 44

Yarn: DK wool in mid-green (A) and fine wool in pale green (B)

METHOD

Pod front * Using A, make 28ch.
1st row (RS) Skip 1ch, 1sc in next ch, 1hdc in next ch, 1dc in next ch, 1tr in next ch, 1dtr in each of next 15ch, 1tr in each of next 2ch, 1dc in each of next 2ch, 1hdc in each of next 2ch, 1sc in next ch, ss in next ch **. Make 20ch. Fasten off invisibly (see page 19).
2nd row Turn work to WS and using a smaller size hook, join B in 1ch at base of pod. Working in the remaining strand of original base ch, ss in each of next 4ch.
1st pea 2ch, turn to RS, inserting hook from right to left ss in top wrap of tr, 2ch, turn to WS and ss in same base ch as before, ss in each of next 4 base ch.
2nd pea [3ch, 2-st tr cluster in same base ch, turn to RS, ss in top wrap of dtr above, 3ch, turn to WS and ss in first of 3ch, then ss in same base ch as before, ss in each of next 4 base ch] 3 times, make last pea as first, ss in each of next 6 base ch. Fasten off invisibly.
Back Work as pod front from * to **. Fasten off invisibly.
Making up Place back underneath pod, edges matching, insert a stiff paper cutout if needed, stitch the two together with backstitch underneath the ch edge on RS. Curl chain stem by twisting it around a pencil.

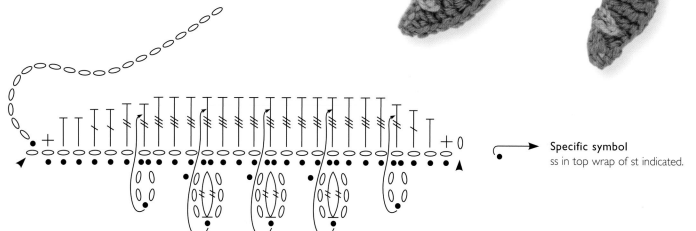

Specific symbol
ss in top wrap of st indicated.

89 FIG LEAF
directory view page 45

Yarn: DK wool

METHOD

Stem Make 14ch, skip 2ch, 1sc in each of next 2ch, ss in each of next 10ch. Do not fasten off.

Leaf

1st round (RS) *1st lobe* 11ch, * skip 3ch, 1dc in each of next 3ch, 1hdc in next ch, 1sc in next ch, 1hdc in next ch, 1dc in next ch, 1tr in next ch. **
2nd lobe 12ch, *** skip 3ch, 1tr in each of next 3ch, 1dc in next ch, 1hdc in next ch, 1sc in next ch, 1hdc in next ch, 1dc in next ch, 1tr in next ch. ****
3rd lobe 14ch, skip 3ch, 1tr in each of next 5ch, 1dc in each of next 4ch, 1hdc in next ch, 1sc in next ch, [3sc in stem of next tr] twice, ss in top ch of stem, turn. Now continue first round in opposite direction:
4th lobe (WS) 11ch, work as first lobe from * to **, ss in first of 3sc in stem of tr of first lobe.
5th lobe 12ch, work as 2nd lobe from *** to ****, ss in first of 3sc in stem of tr of 2nd lobe. Fasten off. From now on work in single remaining strand of ch where necessary, otherwise under 2 strands of each st, including ch.

2nd round (RS) *1st lobe* Rejoin yarn in 2nd ch of first lobe, 1ch, 1sc in next ch, 1hdc in next ch, 1dc in next ch, 1tr in each of next 2ch, 2tr in each of next 5 sts, 1dc in next dc, 1hdc in next dc, 1sc in hdc, ss in each of next 3 sts, skip tr.
2nd lobe Ss in each of next 3ch, 1sc in next ch, 1hdc in next ch, 1dc in next ch, 1tr in each of next 2ch, 2tr in each of next 5 sts, 1tr in next tr, 1dc in next tr, 1hdc in dc, 1sc in hdc, [2-st sc dec in next 2 sts] twice.
3rd lobe 2-st sc dec in next 2ch, 1sc in next ch, 1hdc in next ch, 1dc in each of next 3ch, 1tr in each of next 3ch, 2tr in each of next 5 sts, 1tr in each of next 3 sts, 1dc in each of next 3 sts, 1hdc in next dc, 1sc in next dc, 2-st sc dec in next 2 sts.
5th lobe [2-st sc dec in next 2 sts] twice, 1sc in hdc, 1hdc in dc, 1dc in tr, 1tr in next tr, 2tr in each of next 5 sts, 1tr in each of next 2ch, 1dc in next ch, 1hdc in next ch, 1sc in next ch, ss in each of next 3ch.
4th lobe Skip tr, ss in each of next 3 sts, 1sc in hdc, 1hdc in dc, 1dc in next dc, 2dc in each of next 5 sts, 1dc in each of next 3ch, 1hdc in next ch, 1sc in next ch, ss in next ch. Fasten off invisibly (see page 19).

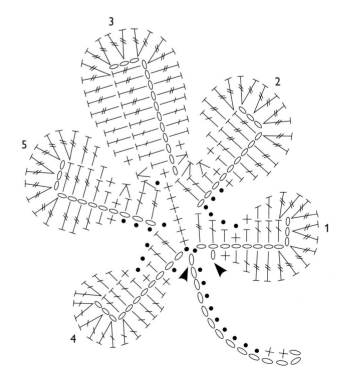

90 HOLLY

directory view page 35, 42

Yarn: DK wool in dark green (A) and fine wool in red (B)

METHOD

Leaf 1st round (RS) Using A, make 12ch, skip 1ch, * 1sc in next ch, 1hdc in next ch, 1dc in next ch, 2dc in next ch, 2tr in next ch, 1tr in next ch, 2tr in next ch, 2dc in next ch, 1dc in next ch, 1hdc in next ch, 1sc in next ch **, 4ch, skip 1ch, ss in next ch, 1sc in next ch, 1ch; working in remaining strand of 11 original base ch, repeat from * to **.

Stem 9ch, skip 1ch, ss in each of next 7ch, 1ch. Continue along sts of first round: *** 1sc in sc, 1sc in hdc, 3ch, skip 1ch, ss in next ch, 1sc in next ch, 1sc in each of next 3 sts, [4ch, skip 1ch, ss in next ch, 1sc in next ch, 1hdc in next ch, skip next st, 1sc in each of next 3 sts] twice, 3ch, skip 1ch, ss in next ch, 1sc in next ch, 1sc in hdc, ss in sc. **** Fasten off invisibly (see page 19).

2nd edge Turn to WS to work along remaining straight edge of first round: join A in 1ch above stem, then work from *** to ****. Do not fasten off. Pin out and press points, then fold leaf along center and on WS, using a smaller size hook and A, work 1sc in each bar of original base ch. Fasten off.

Berry (make 3) Using B, make 4ch, skip 3ch, 4-st tr cluster in first ch, 2ch, from back ss in first ch. Fasten off. Use one yarn end to pad the berry and the other to attach it to the leaf.

91 ORIENTAL POPPY

directory view page 35

Yarn: DK wool in black (A) and red (B)

METHOD

Center Using A, make a slip ring (see page 18).

1st round (RS) 3ch, [2-st dc dec in ring] 8 times, pull end to close ring, ss in top ch of 3ch. 9 sts.

2nd round 3ch, 1dc in each of next 8 sts, with B ss in top ch of 3ch. Continue with B.

First petal

1st row (RS) 1ch, 1sc in each of next 2dc, turn. 3 sts.

2nd row 3ch, 1dc in sc below, 1dc in next sc, 2dc in 1ch. 5 sts.

3rd row 3ch, making last wrap with A 1dc in dc below, with A 1dc in each of next 2dc, making last wrap with B 1dc in next dc, with B 2dc in top ch of 3ch. 7 sts. Continue with B.

4th row 3ch, 1dc in dc below, 1dc in each of next 5dc, 2dc in top ch of 3ch. 9 sts.

5th row 3ch, 2-st dc dec in next 2dc, 3-st dc dec in next 3dc, 2-st dc dec in next 2dc, 1dc in top ch of 3ch. 5 sts. Fasten off invisibly (see page 19).

2nd petal RS facing, join B in next st of center, complete as 1st–5th rows of first petal.

3rd petal As 2nd petal.

Bars to hold remaining 3 petals RS facing and working behind petals, join B in back of center sc at base of first row of one petal, 4ch, [1sc in back of center sc of first row of next petal, 3ch] twice, ss in first ch of 4ch.

4th petal Around next bar work 1ch, 2sc. Complete as 2nd–5th rows of first petal.

5th and 6th petals As 4th petal.

Stamens Thread a wool needle with A and make loops around the center, anchoring them with backstitches. Trim the loops and use the needle to fray the strands of yarn.

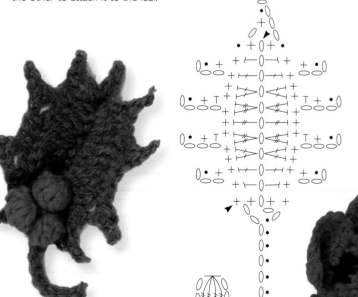

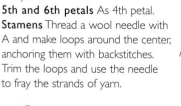

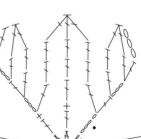

CAMELLIA
directory view page 34

Yarn: DK wool in green (A), yellow (B), and deep pink (C)

METHOD

Center Using A, make a slip ring (see page 18).

1st round (RS) 1ch, 6sc in ring, pull end to close ring. Fasten off invisibly (see page 19). Join B in a sc of first round.

2nd round 1ch, (1sc, 3ch, 1sc) in each sc, remove hook, insert from back in first sc, catch loop and pull through. 6 picots.

3rd round 1ch, [inserting hook from back between 2sc of 2nd round each time, work 1sc in next sc of first round, 1ch] 6 times, ss in 1ch. Fasten off.

First petal Join C in a sc of 3rd round.

1st row (RS) 1ch, 5sc in same sc as join, remove hook, insert from back in same sc of 3rd round, catch loop and pull through. 5 sts.

2nd row 1ch, 2sc in first sc, 1sc in each of next 3sc, 2sc in last sc, remove hook, insert from front in same sc of 3rd round, catch loop and pull through. 7 sts.

3rd row 1ch, 2sc in first sc, 1sc in each of next 5sc, 2sc in last sc, remove hook, insert from back in same sc of 3rd round, catch loop and pull through. 9 sts.

4th row 1ch, 2sc in first sc, 1sc in each of next 7sc, 2sc in last sc, remove hook, insert from front in same sc of 3rd round, catch loop and pull through. 11 sts.

5th row 1ch, 2sc in first sc, 1sc in each of next 9sc, 2sc in last sc, remove hook, insert from back in same sc of 3rd round, catch loop and pull through. 13 sts. Fasten off.

2nd and 3rd petals Leaving 1ch, 1sc, 1ch of 3rd round of center free between petals each time, work as 1st petal.

4th petal Join C in sc between 1st and 2nd petals.

1st row (RS) 1ch, (1sc, 3dc, 1sc) in same sc as join, remove hook, insert from back in same sc of 3rd round, catch loop and pull through. 5 sts.

2nd row 1ch, 2sc in first sc, 1dc in each of next 3dc, 2sc in last sc, insert hook from front in same sc of 3rd round, catch loop and pull through. 7 sts.

3rd row 1ch, 2sc in first sc, 1dc in each of next 5 sts, 2sc in last sc, insert hook from back in same sc of 3rd round, catch loop and pull through. 9 sts.

4th row 1ch, 2sc in first sc, 2dc in each of next 7 sts, 2sc in last sc, insert hook from front in same sc of 3rd round, catch loop and pull through. 18 sts.

5th row 1ch, 2sc in first sc, 1sc in each of next 16 sts, 2sc in last sc, insert hook from back in same sc of 3rd round, catch loop and pull through. 20 sts. Fasten off.

5th and 6th petals Joining C between next 2 petals each time, work as 4th petal.

Specific symbols

┼ sc from back in sc of first round.

●→ Remove hook, insert in sc of 3rd round (from back on RS rows and from front on WS rows), catch loop, and pull through.

93   ROSETTE
directory view page 27

Yarn: DK wool in yellow (A), pink (B), deep pink (C), light wine (D), and dark wine (E)

METHOD

Center Using A, make a slip ring (see page 18).
1st round (RS) 1ch, 6sc in ring, pull end to close ring, ss in 1ch.
2nd round 1ch, 1sc in same sc as join, 3ch, [1sc in next sc, 3ch] 5 times, ss in 1ch. Fasten off invisibly (see page 19).
First ring of petals Join B in a 3ch sp.
1st round * [1ch, 1sc, 3hdc, 1sc] in 3ch sp, remove hook, insert from back in same 3ch sp, catch loop and pull through, remove hook, insert from front in next 3ch sp, catch loop and pull through; repeat from * 5 times more, omitting last pull through to front.
2nd round 1 ch, take hook behind petals, inserting it from back, make 1sc around stem of first sc of 2nd round of center; 3ch, [1sc around stem of next sc of 2nd round of center; 3ch] 5 times, ss in first sc. Fasten off.
2nd ring of petals Join C in a 3ch sp.
1st round * [1ch, 1sc, 1hdc, 3dc, 1hdc, 1sc] in 3ch sp, insert hook from back in same 3ch sp, and pull loop through, remove hook, insert hook from front in next 3ch sp, and pull loop through; repeat from * 5 times, omitting last pull through to front.

2nd round 1 ch, take hook behind petals, inserting it from back, make 1sc around stem of first sc of 2nd round of first ring of petals, 4ch, [1sc around stem of next sc of 2nd round of first ring of petals, 4ch] 5 times, ss in first sc. Fasten off.
3rd ring of petals Join D in a 4ch sp.
1st round * [1ch, 1sc, 1hdc, 1dc, 3tr, 1dc, 1hdc, 1sc] in 4ch sp, insert hook, from back in same 4ch sp, pull loop through, insert hook from front in next 4ch sp, pull loop through; repeat from * 5 times, omitting last pull through.
2nd round 1 ch, take hook behind petals, inserting it from back, make 1sc around stem of first sc of 2nd round of 2nd ring of petals, 5ch, [1sc around stem of next sc of 2nd round of 2nd ring of petals, 5ch] 5 times, ss in first sc. Fasten off.
4th ring of petals Join E in a 5ch sp.
Last round * [1ch, 1sc, 1hdc, 1dc, 5tr, 1dc, 1hdc, 1sc] in 5ch sp, insert hook from back in same 5ch sp, pull loop through, insert hook from front in next 5ch sp, pull loop through; repeat from * 5 times, omitting last pull through. Fasten off.

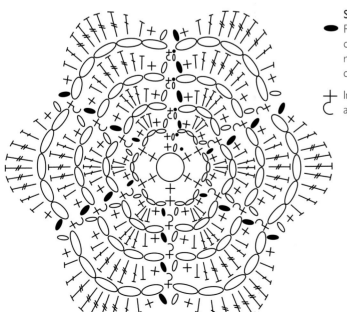

Specific symbols

● Remove hook, insert from back in same ch sp, catch loop and pull through, remove hook, insert from front in next ch sp, catch loop and pull through.

Inserting hook from back, make 1sc around the stem of the st below.

94 RUFFLED ROSE
directory view page 22

Yarn: Fine wool in pale pink (A) and deep pink (B)

METHOD

Using A, make 10ch, join with ss into a ring.
1st round (RS) 7ch, [1tr in ring, 3ch] 9 times, ss in 4th ch of 7ch. 10 ch bars.
2nd round 3ch, 3dc around first 3ch bar, [4dc around next tr; 1dc in center ring, 4dc around next tr; leaving one 3ch bar free work 4dc around next 3ch bar] 4 times, 4dc around next tr; 1dc in ring, 4dc around 4ch, ss in top ch of 3ch. Fasten off invisibly (see page 19).
3rd round Join B around a free 3ch bar, 7ch, [1tr around bar, 3ch] 3 times, * around next 3ch bar work [1tr; 3ch] 4 times; repeat from * 3 times, ss in 4th ch of 7ch. 20ch bars.

4th round 3ch, 3dc around 4ch, 1dc in sp below, [4dc around next tr; leaving one 3ch bar free work 4dc around 3ch bar; 4dc around next tr; 1dc in sp below], 9 times, 4dc around next tr; 4dc around last 3ch bar; ss in top ch of 3ch. Fasten off invisibly. Darn in ends.
5th round This RS round will fold naturally to the back of the rose: rejoin B around a free 3ch bar, 3ch, 2-st tr cluster around bar, [1ch, 3-st tr cluster around next bar] 9 times, 1ch, ss in top ch of 3ch. 10 clusters.
6th round 3ch, [2-st tr cluster in next 2 sts] 10 times, ss in top ch of 3ch. Fasten off leaving an 8in (20cm) end. Run end through top of each cluster and draw up.

Specific symbol
→ Direction of work.

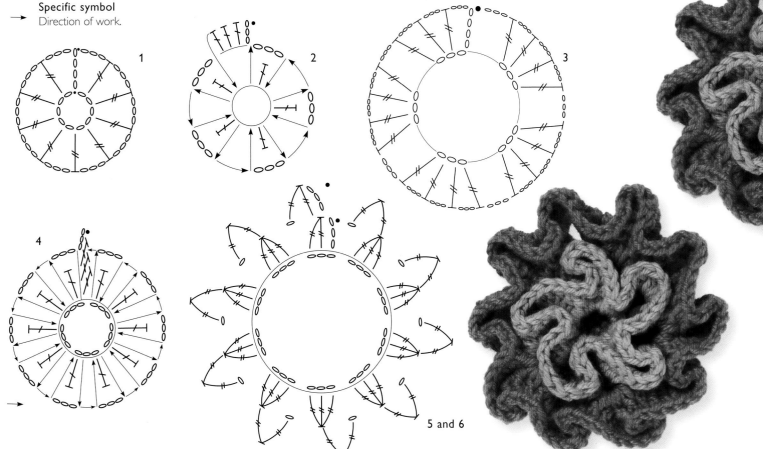

1

2

3

4

5 and 6

95   DIANTHUS
directory view page 27

Yarn: Fine cotton in pink (A), magenta (B), and white (C)

METHOD

Center Using A, make a slip ring (see page 18).
1st round (RS) 3ch, 9dc in ring, pull end to close ring, with B ss in top ch of 3ch. 10 sts. Continue with B.
2nd round 3ch, 1dc in st below, 2dc in each of next 9dc, with C ss in top ch of 3ch. 20 sts. Continue with C.
Petals
3rd round Skip 2dc, * 9tr in next dc, skip 2dc, ss in next dc, take hook behind petal just made and insert from front to back in first dc after petal center, yrh and pull yarn through dc and loop on hook; ** making next 9-st petal in dc immediately after ss of previous petal, repeat from * to ** 4 times, ending 5th petal with ss in the dc before the center of first petal, then take hook behind petal just made and ss in top of first tr of first petal. Fasten off.
4th round Join B in the first tr of a petal, 1ch, [1sc in next tr, 1ch] 8 times, 1sc in ss. Fasten off invisibly (see page 19). Edge each petal in this way.

Specific symbols
Take hook behind petal just made (see 3rd round above).

Final ss of 3rd round (see above).

96   FUCHSIA
directory view page 27

Yarn: Fine cotton in pink (A) and purple (B)

METHOD

Outer flower Using A, make 4ch, join with ss into a ring.
1st round (RS) 3ch, 5dc in ring, ss in top ch of 3ch. 6 sts.
2nd round 2ch, 1sc in st below, 2sc in each of next 5dc, ss in top ch of 2ch. 12 sts.
3rd round 4ch, 1tr in each of next 11sc, ss in top ch of 4ch.
4th round [5ch, 2-st dtr cluster in next tr, 3ch, skip 2ch, ss in next ch, 2-st dtr cluster in next tr, 5ch, ss in next tr] 4 times, ending ss in ss of previous round. Fasten off invisibly (see page 19).
Bell Using B, make 6ch, join with ss into a ring.
1st round (RS) 2ch, 8sc in ring, ss in top ch of 2ch. 9 sts.
2nd round 3ch, 1dc in each of next 8sc, ss in top ch of 3ch.
3rd round 5ch, 1dtr in next dc, [2dtr in next dc, 1dtr in each of next 2dc] twice, 2dtr in next dc, ss in top ch of 5ch. 12 sts. Fasten off invisibly.
Stem Using A, make 15ch, skip 1ch, ss in each of next 14ch. Fasten off.
Stamens Cut 3 short lengths of A, knot the ends and trim.
Making up Sew on stem. Attach bell inside flower, then stamens inside bell.

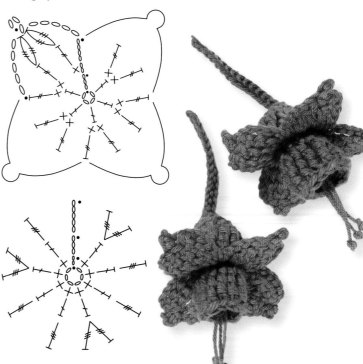

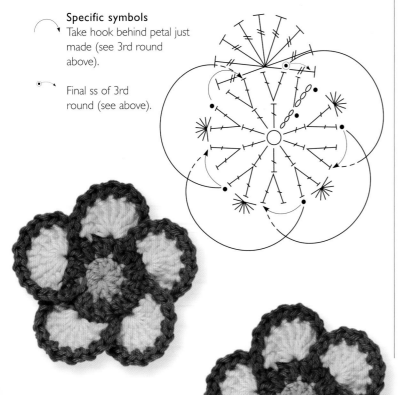

97 FIG
directory view page 45

Yarn: Fine wool in pale green (A) and purple (B)

METHOD

Using A, make a slip ring (see page 18).
1st round (RS) 3ch, 11dc in ring, pull end to close ring, ss to top ch of 3ch. 12 sts.
2nd round 3ch, [2dc in each of next 2dc, 1dc in next dc] 3 times, 2dc in each of next 2dc, ss to top ch of 3ch. 20 sts.
3rd round 3ch, [1tr around front of stem of next dc, 2dc in next dc] 9 times, 1tr around front of stem of next dc, 1dc in ss at base of 3ch, with B ss to top ch of 3ch. 30 sts. Continue with B.
Note: all tr are worked round front of stem.
4th round 3ch, [1tr around stem of next st, 1dc in each of next 2dc] 9 times, 1tr around stem of next st, 1dc in next dc, ss to top ch of 3ch.

5th round 3ch, 1tr around stem of next st, [1dc dec in next 2 dc, 1tr around stem of next st] 9 times, 1dc in next dc, ss to top ch of 3ch. 21 sts.
6th round 3ch, [1tr around stem of next st, 1dc in next dc] 10 times, ss to top ch of 3ch.
7th round 3ch, [1tr-dc dec in next 2 sts] 10 times, ss to top ch of 3ch. 11 sts.
Use coiled B yarn as filler and push it into the fig with the end of a pencil.
8th round 3ch, [1tr around stem of dec] 10 times, ss to top ch of 3ch.
9th round 3ch, [1tr around stem of next st] 10 times, ss to top ch of 3ch.
Fasten off, leaving an end to gather the stitches underneath ribs of last few rows to form the stalk.

Specific symbol
1tr worked around front of stem of st below.

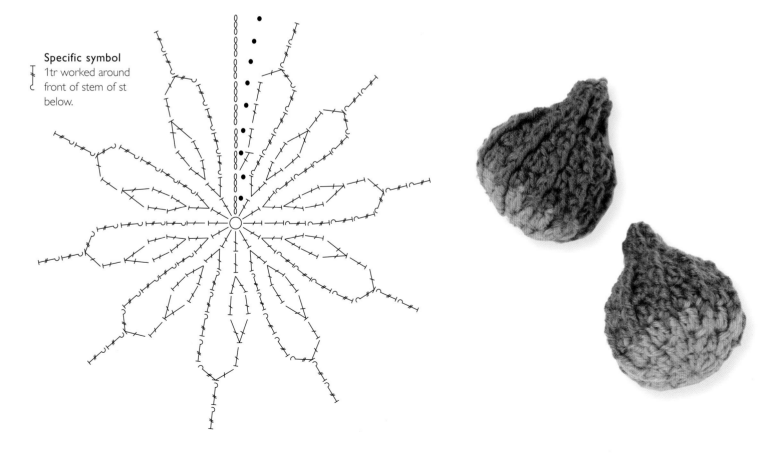

98 **PANSY**
directory view page 30

Yarn: DK wool in yellow (A), purple (B), and mauve (C)

METHOD

Center and first petal Using A, make 6ch, join with ss into a ring.
1st row (RS) 2ch, 2sc in ring, working last wrap with B 1sc in ring. 4 sts. Continue with B.
2nd row 3ch, 1dc in sc below, 2tr in each of next 2sc, 2dc in top ch of 2ch. 8 sts. Fasten off invisibly (see page 19).
3rd row (RS) Join C in base of stem of last dc of previous row, 1ch, 1sc in stem of dc, (1sc, 1ch, 1dc) in top of dc, 1ch, (1tr, 1dtr) in next dc, 2tr in each of next 4tr, (1dtr, 1tr) in next dc, 1ch, (1dc, 1ch, 1sc) in top ch of 3ch, 1sc in next ch, ss in next ch. Fasten off invisibly.
2nd petal Join B in center ch ring.
1st row (RS) 2ch, 2sc in ring. 3 sts.
2nd row 3ch, 1tr in sc below, 1tr in next sc, (1tr, 1dc) in top of 2ch. 5 sts. Fasten off.
3rd row (RS) Join C in base of stem of last dc of previous row, 1ch, 1sc in stem of dc, (1sc, 1ch, 1dc) in top of dc, 1ch, (1tr, 1dtr) in next tr, 1ch, 2tr in next tr, 1ch, (1dtr, 1tr) in next tr, 1ch, (1dc, 1ch, 1sc) in top ch of 3ch, 1sc in next ch, ss in next ch. Fasten off invisibly.

3rd petal As 2nd petal. Darn in all ends.
4th petal With RS facing, join C in first sc in A on first petal, working behind center petals make 4ch, 1sc in base of 2ch of first row of first petal, turn.
1st row (WS) * 4ch, 3tr around ch bar. 4 sts.
2nd row 3ch, 1tr in tr below, 2tr in each of next 2tr, (1tr, 1dc) in top ch of 4ch. 8 sts. Fasten off.
3rd row RS facing, rejoin C in base of first tr of 1st row, 1ch, 1sc in stem of tr, 1sc in top of tr, 1sc in each of first 2ch of 2nd row, (2sc, 1ch, 1dc) in top ch, 1ch, 2tr in next tr, 1tr in each of next 3tr, 2tr in next tr, 1ch, (1dc, 1ch, 1sc) in tr, 3sc in stem of dc, 1sc in each of next 2ch, ss in next ch. Fasten off invisibly.
5th petal With WS facing, join C in ch bar, then work as 4th petal from *.
Making up Press petals separately. Catch together 4th and 5th petals, slightly overlapping 1st and 2nd rows.

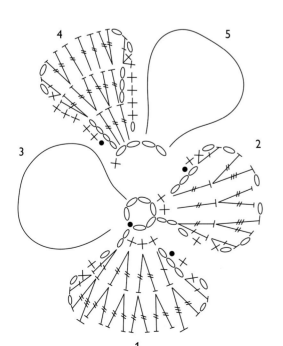

99 VIOLA
directory view page 31

Yarn: Fine wool in yellow (A), mauve (B), and purple (C), single strand embroidery wool in dark olive

METHOD

First petal Using A, make 5ch, join with ss into a ring.
1st row (RS) 3ch, 6dc in ring. 7 sts.
2nd row 5ch, 2-st tr dec in next 2 sts, 1dc in next st, 2-st tr dec in next 2 sts, 5ch, ss in top ch of 3ch. Fasten off invisibly (see page 19).

2nd and 3rd petals
* **1st row** (RS) Join B in 5ch ring, 3ch, 4dc in ring. 5 sts.
2nd row 4ch, 3-st dc dec in next 3 sts, 4ch, ss in top ch of 3ch.
Fasten off invisibly. ** Repeat from * to ** for 3rd petal.
4th petal Turn to WS. Join C in 5ch ring between 1st and 2nd petals, 4ch, ss in ring between 1st and 3rd petals, turn. Now work behind 2nd and 3rd petals:
1st row (RS) 2ch, 6sc around 4ch bar. 7 sts.
2nd row 2ch, 1sc in st below, 1sc in each of next 5sc, 2sc in top ch of 2ch. 9 sts.
3rd row 3ch, 1dc in st below, 1dc in each of next 7sc, 2dc in top ch of 2ch. 11 sts.
4th row 3ch, 4-st dc dec in next 4dc, 3ch, ss in next dc, 2ch, 4-st dc dec in next 4dc, 3ch, ss in top ch of 3ch. Fasten off invisibly.
Making up Press each petal. With embroidery wool make straight sts along line of dc sts, 3 on 1st petal and 2 each on 2nd and 3rd petals.

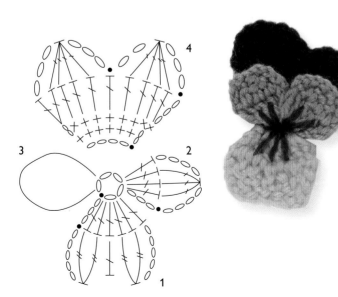

100 CORNFLOWER
directory view page 33

Yarn: DK wool in green (A), deep blue (B), and mid-blue (C)

METHOD

Back Using A and leaving a long end to form stem, make a slip ring (see page 18).
1st round (RS) 1ch, 3sc in ring, pull end to close ring, ss in first sc. 3sc. *
2nd round 1ch, 2sc in each sc, ss in first sc. 6sc.
3rd round 1ch, 1sc in each sc, ss in first sc. Fasten off.
Center Using B, work as back to *, noting that 1st round is now WS.
2nd round 1ch, 2 loop sts in each sc, ss in 1ch. 6 loops.
Joining round With loops facing, place center on back and using B work through one st from each piece each time: 2sc in each pair of sts, ss in first sc. 12 sts. Fasten off.

Florets
First floret With center facing, join C in a sc of joining round.
1st round (RS) 1ch, 5sc in same sc as join, ss in first sc.
2nd round 1ch, 1sc in each sc, ss in first sc.
3rd round 1ch, (1sc, 1dc, 1sc) in each sc, ss in first sc. Fasten off invisibly (see page 19).
Work 6 more florets, placing some next to each other, and spacing others 1 or 2 sc apart to distribute them unevenly around the joining round.

Specific stitch and symbol
 Loop st—insert hook in st, extend left middle finger and catch the strand behind the finger, together with the strand in front of the finger to make a loop, pull both strands through, yrh and pull through 3 loops on hook.

Back

Center

Florets

4 PROJECTS

This chapter contains ideas and suggestions for using the flowers, leaves, fruit, and vegetables from the Directory. These can be used to embellish and accessorize clothing and all kinds of items around the home, enabling you to bring color and even humor to everyday objects, while showcasing your skills. Sewing is the most usual way to attach the items, but pinning or gluing may be more appropriate, depending on your chosen surface.

PROJECT 1:
CLOTHESPIN BAG

A classic clothespin bag made from a wooden coat hanger and
linen tea towels has the snap fastening hidden by a double daisy
knitted in cotton. Happy laundry day!

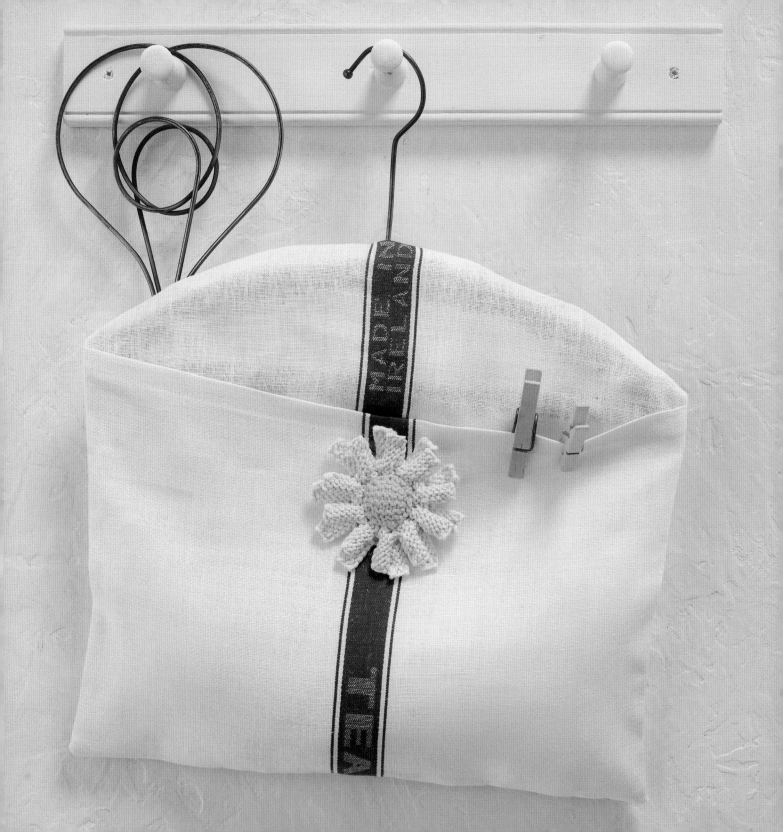

PROJECT 2:
EVENING PURSE

Dressing up a small purse with crochet flowers is both pretty and practical because a rolled rose and small leaf have been added as a zipper pull. This idea could be extended to other tags and zippers.

PROJECT 3: STATIONERY

A loop-and-flower fastening on an address book is an unusual, but attractive way to keep it closed. Here a crochet pansy has been used, but there are lots of alternatives, depending on your preference and of course, your color scheme.

PROJECT 4:
CHRISTMAS GIFT WRAP

Gift wrap is extra luxurious when it's completed with a hand-made flower or leaf. Here, a bright red knitted poinsettia makes an eye-catching and seasonal addition to a present for someone special.

PROJECT 5:
BABY'S CARDIGAN

Tiny crochet forget-me-nots make the gentlest of buttons for a small baby's garment. Another flower that would make a good button is the santolina. Add appliqué crochet meconopsis to complete the look.

PROJECT 6:
WINTER SCARF

Instead of pinning on a brooch, assemble a small bouquet of flowers and stitch it to a plain scarf to cheer up a cold winter's day. This one comprises an auricula, scabious, cornflower, michaelmas daisy, small leaf, and lily of the valley.

PROJECT 7: SUMMER SHOES

Personalize last year's canvas beach shoes or espadrilles with little crochet violas.
Children's and babies' shoes also lend themselves to this sort of decoration.

PROJECT 8: RUFFLES

Echo the gathers of a net skirt or petticoat by attaching a crochet ruffled rose
made with a sparkling yarn. For a young girl's party dress, make the rose in a
soft brushed yarn.

PROJECT 9:
PLACE SETTINGS

Amuse your guests by setting name cards against knitted stalks of asparagus!
It's a crazy idea that looks really rather pretty on the dining table.

PROJECT 10:
SHOPPING BAG

A vintage plastic shopping bag has been given a new lease of life by tying on a small bunch of colorful vegetables—in this case, knitted carrots and crochet peapods. They could make a flamboyant brooch equally well.

INDEX

RESOURCES

Yarn suppliers

Debbie Bliss
Knitting Fever Inc
315 Bayview Avenue
Amityville
New York 11701
tel: 001 516 546 3600
web: www.knittingfever.com

Rowan and Jaeger Yarns Distributor
Rowan c/o Westminster Fibers
165 Ledge Street
Nashua NH 03063
www.westminsterfibers.com

Websites

Many other yarn suppliers and useful
information can be found on the internet.
These are just a few websites:

- www.coatsandclark.com
- www.knitting.about.com
- www.theyarnco.com
- www.uniquekolours.com
- www.yarnsinternational.com

CREDITS

I would like to thank Melody Griffiths and Jan Eaton for the designs they contributed, Susan
Horan for checking the instructions, Simon Pask and Nicki Dowey for their photography, and
everyone at Quarto for their help and encouragement.

Quarto would like to thank the following for supplying images in this book:

- Hannu Liivaar/Shutterstock; 8
- Kathy Burns-Millyard/Shutterstock: 9

All other photographs and illustrations are the copyright of Quarto Inc.